The Textual Diaries of James Joyce

Danis Rose

The Textual Diaries of James Joyce

The Lilliput Press • *Dublin*

The Lilliput Press
4 Rosemount terrace
Arbour Hill
Dublin 7, Ireland

ISBN 1 874675 58 9

Typeset by the Celtic connection
Printed in England by Redwood Books

Contents

III   Technical

Preface

It is a commonplace of criticism, and especially of criticism of biography, that the life of a great writer is his work. This is especially true of James Joyce, whose creative life divides neatly in two: 1903-1922 (oblivion to glory, *Stephen Hero* to *Ulysses*); and 1922-1940 (glory to oblivion, the years of *Finnegans wake*). It is the second part of that curve, the descent, that is the subject of the present work. By means of an analysis of a little-known group of documents, stenographers' copybooks (some fifty odd), known as the *Finnegans wake* notebooks but in reality textual diaries — they elucidate Joyce's thinking over these years, detail the creation of his characters, and contain the distillation of his reading — I tell the story of the composition of *Finnegans wake*, the early confident years, the physical and moral collapse in 1931 (parallelling that earlier period of despair in 1911 when he threw the whole manuscript of *A portrait of the artist* into the fire), and the final painful years when the words came out like drops of blood and seemingly of interest to no-one but himself and his one staunch friend and help-mate, Paul Léon.

A number of factors conspired to occasion the writing of this book. My all-engrossing work on the four-part critical edition of *Finnegans wake* was unexpectedly and inexplicably brought to a halt (temporarily, one hopes) by the interference of the James Joyce Estate (on whose account I began the work), which threatened legal action against my publishers. Because of that interference, my energies and attention have necessarily been drawn into areas quite remote from textual criticism, and the conditions under which I have had to continue to work have been rendered more difficult, both financially and psychologically, than they were before. It is surely ironic that an established text of James Joyce's greatest masterpiece, on which he spent the greater part of his active life, should be subjected to censorship — against which he himself struggled so famously — by his own heirs.

The melancholy reflections which beset me during this period of suspension or abeyance gave rise to a tangential creative impulse. While I awaited a resolution of the *impasse*, I felt, on reading through opinions about the nature of the *Finnegans wake* notebooks and how we should read them, if indeed we should read them at all (for there are some who find their very existence an embarrassment), that the time had come to lift, or try to lift, the cloud of ignorance under which for the most part these matters are being debated. For the present monograph I have accordingly put these all-important documents into chronological order and, using the true sequentiality as a basis of investigation, I tell the story of the formation of *Finnegans wake*, of how it began as another book entirely, *Finn's hotel*, and of how it grew and changed not once, but several times. I describe these notebooks, the material they contain, when and where they were written, and in what order. I also describe the use to which Joyce put their contents. I follow Joyce step by step as he progressed conceptually through his so-called "unreadable" book and in the process demonstrate that despite his genius he was human after all, a writer subject to both error and indecisiveness but, most significantly, that he was always intelligent and intelligible. I do not offer a literary theory but adhere strictly to what is historical and what can be demonstrated from the written evidence. From this analysis a new paradigm of Joyce's last work, I believe, emerges.

This book is in three parts. Part I opens with a prologue describing the tragic fate of Paul Léon, to whom we owe the survival of the notebooks, and continues with a brief account of the history of these texts from the time that they left Joyce's possession up to the present. There follow some comments (equally brief) on previously published scholarly work on the subject. In chapter 3, I present a chronology of the compilation of the notebooks and their relationship with the ongoing *Work in progress*. Part II, the story of *Finnegans wake*, opens with an extended chapter (chapter 4) detailing through an analysis of the first nineteen notebooks the creation of Joyce's "cast of characters" and the relatively rapid composition of the first and third parts of *Finnegans wake*. Mirroring Joyce's progress, the chapter is interrupted midway (at the interface of the description of the eight and ninth notebooks) by a retrospective overview of the episodes already written at the time that Joyce turned to composing the "Four watches of Shaun" (part three of his book). The genesis of these episodes is delineated in the analysis of notebooks 9 to 19. From this point on, with his cast of characters in place and the basic structure of his *Work in Progress* at least outlined, the notebooks necessarily begin to lose their pre-eminent position as witnesses to the evolving design (which position is now taken up more and more by the drafts themselves), although of course they continue to be used in the same manner as before in recording Joyce's immediate thematic concerns and in providing the basic elements (the words) of the text. For this reason, the shorter chapters 5 to 13 which follow describe episode by episode rather than notebook by notebook the more tortuous composition of the remainder of *Finnegans wake*. Part III is somewhat more technical and illustrates in fine detail the current methodology adopted in editing the notebooks. Lastly, two appendixes detail, respectively, Joyce's addresses in the period under consideration and the dates of publication of early versions of *Work in progress*.

The reader needs no previous expertise in Joyce studies other than a sincere interest in *Finnegans wake*. Knowledge of a few facts, however, are of benefit. *Finnegans wake* took Joyce sixteen years to write: its composition was immensely complex and its "manuscript" is more exactly a tangled string of manuscripts involving many thousands of pages and much reworking of drafts. Joyce wrote the book piece by piece as he went along; there was no original all-embracing ground-plan. At the same time he was never careless or casual; he worked with a constraining exactitude — others introduced the confusion. Most importantly, as he worked he filled in the series of notebooks which, though they constitute the source of the words of the text, technically lie outside the main line of the composition itself. The present work is an original ordering of these documents — the textual diaries — and a study of what they reveal. As it turns out, this amounts to the first telling of the story of *Finnegans wake* itself, the story of the stories, all one thousand or one of them, all told. This story is also, of course, the end of his story — James Joyce's.

Danis Rose,
Chapelizod, 4 May 1995

I

General

Prologue:
the lion in the teargarden

[O'Kelly] has been asked by Léon, Joyce's literary manager, to seal up his flat as Léon fears that, the flat not being Joyce's property, the landlord may seize the furniture, which is, for alleged non-payment of rent (*c.* 11.000 frs.). I told Count O'Kelly that he should not accede to this request as Mr. Joyce did not hold an Irish passport and we would have no *locus standi* legally to take such action. He said he would, therefore, refer Léon to the U.S. Embassy. I mentioned that I thought that in such a case the French Law provided for affixing seals pending the appointment of an Administrator.

Cornelius Cremin, Vichy. 16 January 1941

Paul also rescued many things from the Joyce apartment, at great risk to himself. At that time during German occupation, one was at the mercy of a chance informer or of the least indiscretion. The danger lay first in the concierge, but he gave her two hundred francs and told her he was getting some of his own things he had left there and would be back again, since if the proprietor had found out he was after Joyce's things there would have been the devil to pay. The second danger was that of being caught by a German patrol, who were always suspicious of anyone in the street with a pushcart. Paul and a handy-man we someimes employed made two trips with a pushcart, and it was only later I realized how distasteful entering someone else's home and rummaging through

private possessions had been to my husband. He told me he
hoped he had saved everything of importance, and I suggested
that he go once more and make sure. Paul looked at me steadily
and said very gently, "Do you realize what you are saying?"

Lucie Noel (Léon)

Estero Dublin 104. Personal. Monsieur Egli in name of
Society of Swiss Writers Zurich requests intervention if
possible with German authorities in following matter: —
Paul Leon 27 rue Casimir Perrier Paris White Russian Jew,
bearer French Identity Card for Emigres Secretary
Collaboration for years with James Joyce stated arrested as
hostage Paris Stop Society afraid Leon may be shot and that
Joyce's literary heritage thus completely lost as no one else
understood Joyce's works so intimately or could aid so
efficiently with biography Stop Society understands
difficulty of any intervention by Irish Government which I
explained but anxious that request submitted for consideration
Stop Joyce's son also approached me in the matter Stop
Joyce had not Irish passport.

Francis T. Cremins, Berne. 31 October 1941

Eireann Berlin 214. Personal. Society of Swiss Writers
Zurich have informed Cremins that Paul Leon 27 rue Casimir
Perrier Paris White Russian Jew has been arrested by German
Authorities as hostage. Leon was for many years Secretary
Collaborator with James Joyce and Society say no one else
understood his work so well or could aid so effectively with
biography. In case there is danger that Leon be shot please
intervene with Foreign Office on his behalf. Joyce's son also
approached Cremins about him.

Joseph P. Walshe, Dublin. 5 November 1941

Estero Dublin109 S. Personal. Before taking action on your telegram 214 I beg to offer following observations. Recently certain South American representatives here had been instructed by their Government to protest against shooting of hostages, their action was very badly received by German Government Stop At Press Conference it was pointed out this matter was entirely for German Army who must maintain order in occupied territories and take necessary steps to ensure that the shooting of German soldiers will cease. In my opinion there is danger that intervention on behalf of L. might be regarded as interfering in internal German matters where no Irish citizen is involved and might even have some effect on our good relations. I beg to suggest if Department feels we should intervene case might be mentioned to German Minister in Dublin. Please telegraph your observations.

William Warnock, Berlin. 7 November 1941

Eireann Berlin 229. Personal. In view of information in your 109 we agree you should take no action. We shall consider mentioning matter to German Minister.

Joseph P. Walshe, Dublin. 21 November 1941

In the spring Paul was moved to Silesia and murdered by the Germans, presumably on April 4, 1942.

Lucie Noel (Léon)[1]

---

[1]   Sources: Danis Rose and John O'Hanlon, eds, "Ireland and James Joyce", *Joyce studies annual 1992* (Austin: University of Texas Press, 1992); Lucie Noel (Léon), *James Joyce and Paul L. Léon: The story of a friendship* (New York: Gotham Book Mart, 1950).

1 A brief history of the diaries

and, sure, we ought really to rest thankful that we have even
a written on with dried ink scrap of paper at all to show for
ourselves after all it has gone through and by all means
cling to it as with drowning hands, hoping against hope all
the while that things will begin to clear up a bit one way or
another … as they ought to categorically (*protoFW*, 118)

Most but not all of the *Finnegans wake* notebooks — Joyce's
textual diaries — are extant. Of those "fadographs of a yes-
tern scene" missing, it is unlikely that any will re-surface in
the future as they seem to have vanished without trace.
Nineteen pages of words and phrases of slang and colloquial
French have been found amongst the Paul Léon papers in the
National Library of Ireland. These, however, like six similar
pages at Buffalo (catalogued VI.B.49h), were never used by
Joyce. Otherwise, not a single page disassociated from the
conserved set of notebooks has turned up in any of the
recently opened collections. At a 1993 meeting in Paris, Mr
Stephen J. Joyce referred somewhat cryptically to the
continued private existence of a small black notebook dating
from his grandfather's final weeks in Zurich. Such a notebook, if indeed it is not the small memorandum book now at
Buffalo (which anyhow is brown in colour; see the final item
in the chronological list), would provide the full stop to the

sequence as listed below. Had none of the diaries survived, as indeed was almost the case (were it not for the courage, tenacity and wit of Paul Léon, and inexorable fate), it is improbable that the true nature of *Finnegans wake* would ever have been inferred by even the boldest and most astute of critics; it is, moreover, absolutely certain that the book would, in the fullness of its detail, have been closed forever to exegesis. This loss would have been both ours and Joyce's; that he wished his work to be known in all of its parts and its full labyrinthine complexity of assemblage is clear from his fastidious preservation of the documents of its composition — the rough drafts, the fair copies, the marked-up proofs, the printed versions of parts of the text with their new auxesis, the written-on-with-dried-ink galley and page proofs, and so on and — behind these — the textual diaries.

As we shall see, our present knowledge of these notebooks, while today comparatively extensive(they remained available for inspection but virtually unknown until the 1970s), is as yet incomplete — seriously so — and an appreciation of their full intellectual importance awaits the industry of a new generation of textual scholars. This monograph is intended as a retrospective and prospective overview of this massive literary detritus: to consider and set forth what we do know, to repudiate misconceived models and theories, and to delimit what we do not yet know. To begin, however, I turn to the period when James Joyce relinquished personal possession of the notebooks which he had gathered and kept by him throughout a long and bewildering itinerary.

Christmas Eve 1939 found the Joyces in the little village of Saint Gérand-le-Puy in central France. Expecting to return to Paris, they had left behind in their flat on the rue des Vignes all of their possessions: their books, papers, pictures,

furniture and bric-à-brac. France had not yet fallen. Their
initial reason for visiting Saint Gérand was simply to see
their grandson, at the time staying at Maria Jolas's *École
bilingue* in the village. In the event, apart from at least one
flying visit to Paris and a stay of a few weeks in the spring and
early summer at nearby Vichy, they remained for almost a
year. They left for Switzerland on 14 December 1940.

In June 1940 the Germans took Paris and France was
divided. By a stroke of luck, Saint Gérand was just inside the
unoccupied zone. To here, then, a small exodus made its
way: Paul and Lucie Léon, notably, arrived in the village in
the middle of the month. During July and August Joyce
collaborated with Paul on preparing a list of "corrections"
for *Finnegans wake* (principally to the punctuation), which
was then entrusted to Maria Jolas who left for the United
States on 28 August. Life in Saint Gérand, while not perilous,
was incommoding and, besides that, the insistent and
increasing pressure of lack of money precipitated a move.
The Léons decided to return to Paris; Lucie went on 16
August, followed on or about 4 September by her husband.
On re-arrival, Paul resigned from his post as secretary of the
Archives of Philosophy, now under German control, and
almost immediately set about ordering Joyce's affairs. He
sorted and arranged all of his files relating to Joyce — his own
property, it should be noted — which he then encased in nineteen envelopes. He handed these for safekeeping to Count
Gerald O'Kelly, Special Counsellor to the Irish Legation
at Paris, and on 17 January 1941, four days after Joyce's
death, wrote to O'Kelly formally bequeathing the material
to the National Library of Ireland, the papers to be kept
under seal for fifty years.

At a special ceremony held at the National Library on 5

April 1992 and attended by *inter alia* the present author, Albert Reynolds (the Taoiseach), Stephen Joyce and Alexis Léon (Paul's son), these important papers were made available for inspection by the public for the first time. But not quite all. Some were resealed for another fifty-odd years, and others were handed over to Stephen Joyce. This occasioned much controversy. David Norris, a well-known Joycean, raised the matter in the Irish Senate but failed to get any satisfaction. One can, nevertheless, make an educated guess as to the nature of the documents thus effectively consigned to oblivion. In her moving memoir, *James Joyce and Paul L. Léon: the story of a friendship*, published in 1950, Lucie Noel (Lucie Léon) wrote that the envelopes included letters concerning the illness of Joyce's daughter Lucia. It is very likely that it is this material that has been re-sealed. It is also possible that letters concerning the nervous collapse in 1939 of Helen Kastor Joyce, the author's daughter-in-law, were included. If this is the case, then it is likely that these were the papers handed over to Stephen Joyce (Helen's son). Helen left Paris in June 1940, just ahead of the advancing Germans, and returned to the United States where, after a period in a sanatorium, she recovered her health. She was one of the lucky ones. Like Paul Léon she was Jewish, and she might well have shared his terrible fate. In later life, in the 1950s, she became an advisor to the New York-based *James Joyce review*. In earlier, happier times, beginning in or around 1929, she had been one of Joyce's favourite "helpers" and made a contribution to the compilation of the *Finnegans wake* notebooks. Like Paul Léon, Stuart Gilbert, Samuel Beckett and several others, she would read to him, he would stop her, write down in a notebook something that she had read, and ask her to continue.

After he had organized his own files, Paul Léon set about preserving as much as he could of James Joyce's property. He made a number of surreptitious visits to the Joyce flat in the rue des Vignes (the rent was outstanding) and recovered most of the important material. Léon's peregrinations through the streets of Paris with a pushcart constituted a grim re-enactment fifty years after — the same anew — of James Joyce, his father and his brothers, trundling a pushcart through the streets of Dublin in an attempt to evade another unpaid landlord. Later, on 7 March 1941, the Léons attended an auction of Joyce's furniture and other effects held (strictly illegally) by the proprietor of the flat. Paul's knowledge of what was important enabled him to buy back most of the valuable items, especially the books, using money provided by Lucie Léon's brother, Alec Ponisovsky. Everything thus collected by Léon was stored in Paris, some with friends, some with a lawyer, and ultimately returned to Nora Joyce after the War.

The most important papers and documents (including contracts) were put into a large brown suitcase. It is probable that the notebooks (with the exception of the last one or two which Joyce had by him in Saint Gérand and took with him to Switzerland) were placed in this suitcase. It remained in the Léon flat at 27 rue Casimir-Périer until 1942 and narrowly escaped confiscation. Before Paul's arrest on 21 August 1941, the apartment was visited by the Gestapo on three occasions, and thoroughly searched twice. The brown suitcase was not found.

Several years were to pass before the notebooks were to appear in public, at a time when the author's son, George Joyce, chose to realize what capital he could by the disposal of his patrimony. A commemorative exhibition was opened in October 1949 at the La Hune Gallery in Paris, and negotiations for the sale of the items on display (which included the notebooks) were conducted discreetly behind the scenes. The eventual purchaser was the Lockwood Memorial Library of the University of Buffalo, who used money provided *ex dono* Margaretta E. Wickser.[1]

In 1977/1978 a complete set of photo-replicates of all of the surviving notebooks was made available for study in the monumental *James Joyce archive*, with prefatory material by Danis Rose (vols 28, 35-43) and David Hayman (vols 29-34).[2] While, owing to the cost, these volumes are out of the reach of most individuals, they have been purchased by many of the major libraries and are thus much more immediately accessible than the originals at Buffalo. This has enabled preliminary research to be carried out almost at leisure and has greatly advanced general scholarly awareness of the extent and import of the material, of which the bulk remains unedited.

---

[1]   For a full description of the material, see Peter Spielberg, comp., *James Joyce's manuscripts and letters at the University of Buffalo: a catalogue* (Buffalo: University of Buffalo Press, 1962).
[2]   The extremely useful lists of colour codes which are included at the end of each volume are the work of Michael Groden.

2 Editions

Quand il [Michel-Ange] sortit de la chapelle, il dut marcher
au hasard, incapable de regarder à ses pieds, et longtemps
il ne put lire une lettre qu'en la tenant en l'air.
                              Edouard Devoghel, *Le Vatican* (1927)[1]

⊓ can't see feet, read letter in air
                              James Joyce, notebook VI.B.4 (1929)

To date, only three comprehensive editions of the copybooks
archivally catalogued as *"Finnegans wake* notebooks" have
appeared in print. Of this trinity, the first, published in 1961
under the title *Scribbledehobble*,[2] is strictly speaking not an
"original" notebook at all, but rather a repository of notes
drawn from other notebooks. The third, published in 1989
under the title *The lost notebook*[3] (the edition, as it happens, is a reconstruction recreated from diverse textual
evidence in the manuscripts and from an extant, partial

[1] "When Michelangelo left the chapel, he had to walk at random,
incapable of looking at his feet, and for a long time he could read a letter
only when he held it in the air." This particular source was discovered by
Ingeborg Landuyt in 1994.
[2] James Joyce, *Scribbedehobble: the ur-workbook for Finnegans wake*,
ed. Thomas E. Connolly (Evanston: Northwestern University Press, 1961).
[3] James Joyce, *The lost notebook*, ed. Danis Rose and John O'Hanlon
(The Split Pea Press, Edinburgh, 1989).

transcription), is actually a notebook compiled by Joyce for use in the writing of *Ulysses* and bears the provenance "Zurich 1917".

A pioneering effort, *Scribbledehobble* was brought out before any significant scholarly work had been done on the *Finnegans wake* notebooks. While this transcription includes references to the text of *Finnegans wake* for the majority of those elements used, it contains almost no annotation of the notes themselves and no attempt is made to identify their origin. For this and other reasons, the edition (a handsome volume set in Bell Roman) has had a regrettable negative gravitational effect on subsequent notebook studies. The self-styled ur-notebook is, rather ironically, atypical, and is in fact structured according to a system devised for *Ulysses*. In it, preparatory to anything else and before entering a single note, Joyce listed headings or titles neatly disposed every 10, 20 or 30 pages or so. In addition to the names of the episodes of *Ulysses*, the titles of all of his earlier published work from "Chamber Music" to "Exiles" are included. Although the titles themselves possibly date from 1922, the bulk of the first batch of notes entered dates from the summer of 1923. The structure, the assumption of a 1922 date for the notes and the lack of annotation for those notes has led commentators to assume that after he had finished *Ulysses* Joyce embarked on an "extended meditation" of his earlier work. There is no real evidence for this view as the notes themselves, when looked at objectively, bear only an implausible thematic connection, at best, with the titles under which they are arranged, and do not in any conceivable way constitute a "meditation". A second fatal error in the edition was the editor's assumption (fair enough in the circumstances) that a cluster of notes found near the end of the notebook (see the entry "SD2" in the chronological list which follows) were instrumental in drafting the first and fifth chapters of *Finnegans wake* (I.1 and I.5). This led Connolly and all other commentators after him (including, it should be said, the present writer in a previous incarnation) to assume an early date (1926) for the inscription of these notes. In fact, as John O'Hanlon has only recently confirmed, the material was written no earlier than the autumn of 1931. In a rare reversal of the usual notebook-draft sequence and with the end in view (effected in many cases) of implanting echoes and recurrences elsewhere in the text, the elements were in fact taken out of *Work in progress* and written into the notebook and not, as even the most normally attentive of us would suppose, the other way round.

Although fascinating in its own right (it details, among other things, Joyce's initial construction of the verisimilar background for Bloomsday, 16 June 1904), *The lost notebook* is strictly speaking a *Ulysses* document and not therefore pertinent to the present study other than as a model for the reconstruction of the ten (if not more) non-extant *Finnegans wake* notebooks. The recovery of notebooks lost or missing in action, arcane as the pursuit might seem, is a necessary part of a comprehensive exploration of the art of James Joyce.

The index manuscript, the first edition of a true-to-type *Finnegans wake* notebook — comprehensive and ambitious, if crudely printed — was published in 1978.[1] While producing a complete annotated edition of the notebook, my main intention in this work was an illustration of a composite hypothesis of the nature of the material entered in the

---

[1] James Joyce, *The index manuscript: Finnegans wake holograph workbook VI.B.46*, ed. Danis Rose (Colchester: A Wake Newslitter Press, 1978).

notebooks as a set; their intimate symbiosis with *Finnegans wake*; and, the nature of the beast, *Finnegans wake* itself. VI.B.46, a notebook dating from late 1937/early 1938 and as such one of the last to be compiled, was selected for this purpose not because the notebook was distinct in type from its fellows but simply because it was at the time that one on which I had gathered the most information and on which most work had been done by other scholars. The arguments as to the fundamental nature of both the text of *Finnegans wake* and the extra-textual material contained in the notebooks were outlined in a General Introduction and crystallized in three logically separate propositions: in modern parlance, in a theoretical matrix, which we can profitably repeat here.

1.   Finnegans wake *is primarily an ordered assemblage of units (words and phrases) taken from the notebooks.*

Comments :

(a)   By a "unit" is signified a word or words comprising a single entry or "element": thus both "miseffectual" (VI.B.11:32; *FW* 118.28) and "I rose up one morning and looked in the glass" (VI.B.33:28; *FW* 249.26) are equally single units.

(b)   Occasionally the unit as it appears in translocation in the drafts of *Finnegans wake* is a linguistic distortion of the original in the notebook: thus the concatenation must at times be critically established. For example, "finger = 15 lbs" (VI.B.27:50) reappears in the final text in the variant form "his pig indicks weg femtyfunt funts" (*FW* 241.09).

(c)   Each integral part of the final text of *Finnegans wake*, such as a paragraph, was most generally effected not at one time of writing but incrementally by a staggered series of expansions of a root sentence or sentences. Occasionally, increasing linguistic distortion of the original text accompanied this process of accretion.

(d)   It may reasonably be inferred that the function of the linguistic distortion was in part to permit the conjugation of otherwise irreconcilable units.

2. *The notebooks are primarily compilations of units derived from external sources.*

Comments :

(a)   By an "external source" is intended a book, a magazine article, a pamphlet, a newspaper, or some other printed work. Thus the words "from older sources" appearing in the text of *Finnegans wake* at 30.5 and taken from notebook VI.B.3:158 derive directly from the sentence

> "One invasion followed another and an Irish historical tract written *c.* A.D. 721 and copied from older sources gives the definitive Gaelic monarchy as beginning contemporaneously with Alexander the Great in the 4th century B.C."

which appears on page 29 of *Ireland in the making of Britain*, by Benedict Fitzpatrick (London, 1922).

(b)   A very small part of the content of the notebooks is exceptional to the above rule. For example, one sometimes encounters numerical calculations, addresses, telephone numbers and the like, which clearly do not belong to the note-taking properly. Also, very occasionally, a short section of text is *drafted* on a notebook page.

3. *The translation of each unit from notebook to draft was intermediated by referring that unit to one of a small number of contextual invariants.*

Comments :

> This last, rather clipped and cryptic assertion is discussed at length in chapter 4 of the present study. Put simply, what it says is that Joyce first associated (either explicitly in the notebook itself or implicitly in the act of transference) the unit with one or other of the characters or sets of characters of his book. In a real sense it is no more than a development of the procedure which Hugh Kenner aptly described as the "Uncle Charles principle":[1] the Joycean text characteristically takes on the accent and the attributes (the resonance) of that which is being written about.

When one considers the essentially subversive nature of this metacritic — to put it uncircumscribedly, I claimed rather radically that *Finnegans wake*, famously the world's most idiosyncratic, eccentric and creative work, is in truth an *assemblage* made up of bits and pieces of sentences freely plagiarized by Joyce from the writings of other men and women (and with wild abandon as to the proprieties of copyright), and that one of the main reasons for the setting into motion of his Wholesale Safety Pun Factory was to ensure that the whole thing made sound English sense — one would have thought (the author in his prelapsarian innocence certainly thought so) that the publication of *The index manuscript* in 1978 would have far-reaching consequences for Joyce scholarship. The hypotheses were not simply

[1]   Hugh Kenner, *Joyce's voices* (London: Faber and Faber, 1978), p.15.

dogmatically stated : they were supported by a string of edited "indexes" (an "index" being a section of a notebook deriving from a common, single source). In keeping with scientific procedure, the hypotheses were objective and *falsifiable*: they were either true or not true and could be demonstrated to be one or the other. It simply required further research more exhaustively to investigate the assertions.

As it happened, nothing happened. For the greater number of Joyce scholars *Finnegans wake* remained, and remains, a book of the dark, scarcely read and scarcely readable.

More recently, the hypotheses have been critically validated and the exegetic system proposed followed in scores of articles by a new generation of textual scholars: indeed, the paradigm inherent in *The index manuscript*, with its indexes, units and transferrals, today forms the bedrock of progressive *Finnegans wake* notebook exegesis.[1]

---

[1] There has since the early seventies been a steady stream of relevant notebook-oriented articles published in the different journals and in volumes of collected essays, particularly in the now discontinued *A wake newslitter* (1962-1980) and the *Finnegans wake circular* (1985-present). In addition, David Hayman makes extensive use of the notebooks in his *The wake in transit* (Ithaca: Cornell University Press, 1990).

3 The space-time axis: a chronology of the notebooks

Ulysses, Joyce's "chaffering allincluding most farraginous chronicle", was finally put aside by him (if we discount his minor revisions in 1936 for the English edition) on or about 31 October 1922 when he abruptly and inchoately ended his spot correcting of the printed text.[1] Such errata as he listed for *Ulysses* (and wonderfully inadequate they were too) he entered in a child's small copybook (now in the British Library), at the back of which he first, and then his daughter, Lucia, jotted down the names of those persons to whom he wished Harriet Weaver to send copies of her leaflet on *Ulysses*. He forwarded the copybook to Miss Weaver on 3 November, noting that it contained his "list of corrections pages 1 to 290".[2] However, on inspecting the notebook sent to Miss Weaver, one sees immediately that the corrections listed pertain to pages 1 to 258 of *Ulysses*. Corrections for the remaining pages 259-290 were for some reason (and not for lack of paper space) entered in a second notebook. That this second notebook (catalogued by Spielberg as VI.B.10 and

---

[1] For a fuller discussion see Danis Rose and John O'Hanlon, "A Nice beginning: on the *Ulysses/Finnegans wake* interface", *European Joyce studies*, 2, 165-173 (Amsterdam/Atlanta, Ga.: Rodopi, 1990).
[2] Joyce lifted his own shaggy brow from the pages of *Ulysses* for the last time midway through the "Cyclops" episode, precisely at the valediction: "He is gone from mortal haunts: O'Dignam, sun of our morning. Fleet was his foot on the bracken: Patrick of the beamy brow. Wail, Banba, with your wind: and wail, O ocean, with your whirlwind."

by his reckoning the tenth or eleventh of the post-*Ulysses* notebooks to have been written) is in fact the most original of the so-called *Finnegans wake* notebooks has now been established (Rose and O'Hanlon, *supra*). Moreover, Spielberg's *ascription* is in a sense also mistaken, as the *Wake* was not yet conceived of at the time of compilation of the notebook.

Either there were no obvious errors in pages 259 to 281 of *Ulysses* or a page of VI.B.10 was removed and lost, for it contains corrections for pages 282 to 288 only: a mere six corrections in all. (In the event, these were forgotten.) Immediately thereafter, with *Ulysses* behind him, Joyce began and continued to enter notes intended, one presumes, for a new book, but one that had not yet germinated in his mind. Thus begun, Joyce's notetaking continued unabated for most of the rest of his life, through the years of *Finn's hotel* and *Finnegans wake*,[1] leaving us with an almost perfect record of his literary concerns (imperfect only in that we are quite certain that some of the notebooks he compiled in the period are lost); but, before one can begin to follow the changing curve of these concerns and to chronicle the details of his engagement, one must first arrange the notebooks into a strict chronological order. As the notebooks are undated and unnumbered by Joyce, this is less simple an undertaking than might appear on first inspection; and, indeed, given the

[1] Joyce's first idea for a book to follow *Ulysses* was for a series of short texts based on Irish historical and mythological themes. These he composed in 1923 under the title "Finn's hotel". In late 1923-early 1924 he changed his mind and, laying aside the short texts, began instead to write the long continuous work that eventually became *Finnegans wake*. For a fuller account, see the Afterword to my edition of *Finn's hotel*, which I hope to publish in 1995 as the first volume of the critical edition of *Finnegans wake*.

implications of the precise arrangement one might arrive at, it has proved quite a controversial one.

There are 49 extant primary notebooks (VI.B.1-48 and VIII.C.2 in Spielberg's classification).[1] In addition, there are 18 transcriptions (VI.C.1-18) of a number of the notebooks. Included in this set of transcriptions are copies of undeleted material in seven lost primary notebooks. Two of these (VI.-D.4 and 7), however, date from the *Ulysses* period.

The earliest systematic attempt to classify the notebooks was made by Peter Spielberg in 1962. While on the faculty of the University of Buffalo he devoted three years to cataloguing all of the letters and manuscripts of James Joyce held in the University's Lockwood Memorial Library. With regard to the notebooks, Spielberg makes no pretence at definitiveness, yet his arrangement, while quite a flawed one, has hitherto sufficed. The second attempt to date (but not to classify) the notebooks was made by Roland McHugh in 1972 in *A wake newslitter*. Although an improvement on Spielberg, McHugh's recension was again seriously inadequate. In the course of writing prefaces to volumes 28-43 of the *James Joyce archive* in 1977, David Hayman and Danis Rose discussed Spielberg's and McHugh's dating and suggested many improvements. This work, however, did not constitute a thorough reclassification.

The present sorting and dating of the notebooks is the only one which takes seriously the idea — first mooted by Spielberg — that the set of notebooks as a whole constitute a continuous sequence of notetaking. While there is some overlapping among the notebooks, it is the exception rather than the rule. With the publication of the rearranged drafts,

[1]   VI.B.49 is a collection of loose pages. VI.B.50 is little more than a sheaf of loose sheets.

typescripts and proofs of *Finnegans wake* (volumes 44-63 of the *Archive*), and in fuller consideration of the internal evidence provided by the notebooks themselves (with reference to published and unpublished letters of Joyce and his associates), it has been found possible to order the notebooks in the sequence of their composition and, further, to indicate the lacunae in the sequence.[1] For reasons that are obvious, the corrected enumeration given below should replace Spielberg's classification. It is followed hereafter in the present study. The dates cited are as exact as we can make them at this time, though it should be possible further to refine them when the notebooks are finally and fully edited.

In the new ordering given below, the number, date and provenance of each notebook is first listed. This is followed by a brief physical description (the page measurements are approximate) and an indication of "first use". By this is meant the compositional work on which Joyce was engaged at the time of compilation of the notebook. A compact history of the writing of *Finns's hotel/Finnegans wake* is thereby included and should prove useful to scholars. It should be pointed out, however, that the notebooks were not used only (or even principally) at the time of their compilation, but were also resorted to by Joyce at later times to complement current notes.

In addition to the forty-nine extant notebooks, ten missing notebooks are listed. Five of these (VI.D.1-3, 5-6) were transcribed in part in the mid-1930s by France Raphael. Another five (designated VI.X.1-5) are either entirely missing or exist only in small fragments.

[1]   This research was carried out by John O'Hanlon and Danis Rose over the last few years while engaged on completing the critical edition of *Finnegans wake* and is set out here for the first time.

To complete the picture, several groupings of "recycled" notes are included in the listing. These include: VI.A ("Scribbledehobble"), which consists of four parts: SA (the handwriting "A" notes), SB (the handwriting "B" notes), SD1 (the first part of the handwriting "D" notes) and SD2 (the second part of the handwriting "D" notes); the six sheafs of worksheets (Sheets I-VI); and, finally, the Raphael transcriptions (the VI.C notebooks). There is, in addition, recycled matter in the primary notebooks themselves (the "N" series); thus, for example, there are notes from N51 (VI.B.44) and N52 (VI.B.42) which Joyce copied into N53 (VI.B.46). Of greater interest are the notes taken from Joyce's *texts* (drafts and early publications) of *Work in progress* and found in the notebooks. Such material is found, for example, in N13 (VI.D.3), N15 (VI.D.2), SD2, N48 (VI.B.38) and N50 (VI.B.37). The purpose evidently was to facilitate the creation of recurrent motifs. Revealingly, apart from *FH v* (the "Earwicker" vignette which was the starting-off point for *Finnegans wake* proper), there is no evidence in the notebooks of any material from the other sections of *Finn's hotel* being used in this way.

Chronological order of Notebooks

Key: FH = *Finn's hotel*; FW = *Finnegans wake*. Note also that *Finnegans wake* is divided into four parts (also called "Books"), I, II, III and IV; part I consists of eight episodes or chapters (I.1-I.8), part II of four (II.1-II.4), part III of four (III.1-4), and part IV of one (IV). In addition, the episodes divide into sections (denoted by "§").

N1 (VI.B.10) late Oct 1922-Jan 1923: Nice, Paris.
120 pages unruled paper 21 x 12.8 cm.; pages missing.
First [contemporaneous] use: *Ulysses* errata, random
notetaking.

N2 (VI.X.1) late Jan-early Mar 1923: Paris
Missing notebook.
First use: random notetaking, preliminary notes for FH.

N3 (VI.B.3) Mar-Jul 1923: Paris, London, Bognor.
172 pages unruled paper 21 x 13.3 cm.; some pages torn.
First use: FH.

SA (VI.A, handwriting A) probably Jul 1923: Bognor.
Recycled matter. It is possible that material from N2 (VI.X.1)
is included in this part of VI.A.
First use: FH.

N4 (VI.B.25) Jul-Aug 1923: Bognor, London, Paris.
102 pages unruled paper 21 x 13.2 cm.; most pages torn,
some missing. Material from the torn and missing pages can
be found in SD1 pages 31-45 (see below).
First use: FH.

N5 (VI.B.2) late Aug-late Sep 1923: Paris, Tours, Paris.
180 pages unruled paper 18.5 x 13.5 cm.; some pages torn or
missing.
First use: FH.

N6 (VI.B.11) late Sep-late Nov 1923: Paris.
170 pages unruled paper 20.7 x 13.2 cm.; some pages missing.
First use: FW I.2 and I.3 first drafts.

N7 (VI.X.2) Dec 1923: Paris
Missing notebook. VI.B.49e — 2 pages unruled paper 20 x
12 cm — probably belongs to this notebook.
First use: FW I.3-I.5 early drafts.

N8 (VI.B.6) Jan-Feb 1924: Paris.
192 pages unruled paper 20.7 x 13.2 cm.; some pages missing.
VI.B.49c — 2 pages — probably belongs to this notebook.
First use: FW I.5-I.8 early drafts.

N9 (VI.B.1) late Feb-Apr 1924: Paris.
180 pages unruled paper 21 x 13.2 cm; some pages torn.
First use: FW I.8, revision of "Mamalujo" for *Transatlantic
review*, III.1 early drafts.

N10 (VI.B.16) Apr-May 1924: Paris.
146 pages unruled paper 19.4 x 13.6 cm.; some pages missing.
First use: FW III.1-III.2 early drafts.

N11 (VI.B.5) mid May-late Jul 1924: Paris, Brittany.
162 pages graph paper 20.9 x 13.4 cm.; some pages missing.
First use: FW III.1-III.2 early drafts.

N12 (VI.B.14) Aug-late Nov 1924: Brittany, Paris, London,
Paris.
232 pages graph paper 17.3 x 11 cm.
First use: FW III.1-III.3 early drafts.

N13 (VI.D.3) early Dec 1924-Feb 1925: Paris.
Missing notebook (see VI.C.4 220-280, VI.C.5 1-91 for
partial copy).
First use: FW III.3 early drafts, revision of III.1-3.

N14 (VI.B.7) Mar-mid Apr 1925: Paris.
240 pages graph paper 14.7 x 9.5 cm.
First use: revision of FW I.2 and I.5 for *Contact collection*
and *Criterion*.

N15 (VI.D.2) mid Apr-May 1925: Paris.
Missing notebook (see VI.C.3 178-242 and also VI.C.15
177-252 for partial copy).
First use: revision of FW I.2 for *Contact collection*.

N16 (VI.D.1) May-Jun 1925: Paris.
Missing notebook (see VI.C.2 123-197 for partial copy).
First use: general notetaking.

N17 (VI.B.9) Jun-early Jul 1925: Paris
154 pages graph paper 17.8 x 10.4 cm.; many pages torn out
and missing.
First use: revision of FW I.7 and I.8 for *This quarter* and
Calendar/Navire d'argent.

N18 (VI.B.8) late Jul-Sep 1925: Northern and Western France.
240 pages graph paper 16.8 x 10.9 cm.
First use: revision of FW I.8 for *Navire d'argent*, III.4 early
drafts.

N19 (VI.B.19) Jun-early Jul, and Sep-late Nov 1925: Paris
228 pages graph paper 16.6 x 10.6 cm.
First use: revision of FW I.7 for *This quarter*, III.4 early
drafts.

SB (VI.A handwriting B) probably Fall 1925: Paris.
Recycled matter from notebook N14 (VI.B.7).

N20 (VI.B.13) Dec 1925-early Mar 1926: Paris.
232 pages graph paper 16.7 x 10.5 cm.; some pages missing.
First use: FW III.4 early drafts, revision of III.1-3.

N21 (VI.B.20) Mar-Apr 1926: Paris.
116 pages graph paper 21.7 x 8.4 cm.
First use: FW III.2 interlude ("Dave the Dancekerl"), revision of III.1-3.

N22 (VI.B.17) Apr-May 1926: Paris.
108 pages ruled paper 20.9 x 13 cm.
First use: revision of FW III.1-4.

N23 (VI.B.12) Jun-Aug 1926: Paris.
192 pages ruled, lined paper 21.5 x 13.7 cm.
First use: revision of FW III.1-4, early drafts of II.2§8 (the "triangle").

N24 (VI.D.5) Aug-Sep 1926: Belgium.
Missing notebook (see VI.C.8 217-end, VI.C.9 1-19; and also VI.C.10 249-end, VI.C.16 1-65).
First use: FW II.2§8 early drafts, I.1 early drafts.

N25 (VI.B.15) late Sep 1926-late Jan 1927: Paris.
224 pages graph paper 19.1 x 12.5 cm.
First use: FW II.2§8 drafts, I.1 drafts.

N26 (VI.B.18) Mar-Jul 1927: Paris, Holland, Paris.
286 pages ruled paper 21.4 x 13.3 cm.; some pages missing.
First use: revision of FW I.2-I.5 for *transition*, I.6 early draft.

N27 (VI.X.3) Summer 1927: Paris.
Missing notebook. VI.B.49d — 2 pages graph paper 18 x 10.7 cm. — probably belongs to this notebook.
First use: preparation of FW I.6 for *transition*.

N28 (VI.D.6) Fall-Winter 1927: Paris.
Missing notebook (see VI.C.11 96-217 for partial transcription).
First use: revision of FW I.7-I.8 for *transition*, and I.8 for *Anna Livia Plurabelle*.

N29 (VI.B.21) Jan-Apr 1928: Paris, Normandy, Paris.
300 pages ruled, lined paper 20.7 x 13.4 cm.
First use: revision of FW II.2§8 for *transition*, III.1 for *transition*, and I.8 for *Anna Livia Plurabelle*.

N30 (VI.B.22) May-late Jun 1928: South of France, Paris.
188 pages graph paper 18.9 x 11.5 cm. VI.B.49g, 2 pages blue stationery 26.7 x 20.7 cm., contains notes contemporaneous with this notebook.
First use: revision of FW I.8 for *Anna Livia Plurabelle*, III.2 for *transition*.

N31 (VI.B.26) Jul-Sep 1928: Austria, Paris.
184 pages ruled, lined paper 24.9 x 9.3 cm.
First use: general notetaking.

N32 (VI.B.23) 1928 Sep-Dec: Le Havre, Paris.
156 pages unruled, heavy paper 17.8 x 12.5 cm.
First use: revision of FW III.3 for *transition*.

N33 (VI.B.4) Jan-late Apr 1929: Paris.
336 pages ruled, lined paper 21.2 x 13.2 cm.

First use: revision of FW III.3 for *transition*, I.6§3, II.2§8 and III§IC for *Tales told of Shem and Shaun*.

N34 (VI.B.27) May-July 1929: Paris, England.
156 pages unruled, heavy paper 17.4 x 12.1 cm.
First use: revision of FW I.6§3, II.2§8 and III§IC for *Tales told of Shem and Shaun*, III.4 for *transition*.

N35 (VI.B.24) Aug 1929-early Feb 1930: England, Paris.
300 pages ruled, lined paper 20.9 x 13.2 cm.; some pages missing.
First use: revision of III.4 for *transition*; III§3B for *Haveth childers everywhere*.

N36 (VI.B.29) Feb-late Mar 1930: Paris.
224 pages ruled, lined paper 20.4 x 13 cm. VI.B.49f, 2 pages unruled paper 26.9 x 20.8 cm., contains notes gathered for this notebook.
First use: revision of III§3B for *Haveth childers everywhere*.

N37 (VI.B.28A) late Mar-early Apr 1930: Paris.
First 9 pages of this notebook; ruled, lined paper 18.9 x 12.3 cm.
First use: revision of III§3B for *Haveth childers everywhere*.

N38 (VI.B.32) May-Oct 1930: Zurich, Paris, England, Étretat, Paris.
232 pages ruled, lined paper 21.1 x 13 cm.
First use: notes for FW II.1

N39 (VI.X.4) Nov-Dec 1930: Paris, Zurich, Paris.
Missing notebook; brown cover (described in unpublished

letters to Paul Léon dated 15 and 28 Aug 1932). The thematically related material at the beginning of SDI (see below) is possibly from this notebook.
First use: FW II.1 early drafts.

N40 (VI.B.28B) Jan-Feb 1931: Paris.
Final 191 pages of this notebook; ruled, lined paper 18.9 x 12.3 cm.
First use: notes for FW II.1 (none used).

N41 (VI.B.33) late Feb-early Apr 1931: Paris.
200 pages ruled, lined paper 20.7 x 13.2 cm.
First use: notes for FW II.1, II.1 early drafts.

SD1 (VI.A.1-20, 22-47) early March 1931: Paris.
Recycled matter from earlier notebooks.
First use: FW II.1 early drafts

N42 (VI.B.31) late Apr-Nov 1931: England, Paris.
272 pages ruled, lined paper 20.9 x 13.3 cm.
First use: revision of Book I *transitions* (first set).

SD2 (VI.A.744-762) Oct-Nov 1931: Paris.
Recycled matter from text of Book I *transitions*.
First use: revision of Book I *transitions* (first set).

N43 (VI.B.35) early and late 1932: Paris, Zurich, Paris.
146 pages ruled paper 20.8 x 13.2 cm.; some pages missing. VI.B.49b, 2 pages unruled paper 21 x 15.7 cm, contains a continuation of notes entered in this notebook. VI.B.49a, 1 page unruled paper 19 x 15.1 cm., contains notes compiled contemporaneously with this notebook.

First use: revision of FW Book I *transitions* (second set), II.1 for *transition*.

Sheets I late 1932: Paris.
Recycled matter from notebooks.
First use: revision of FW II.1 for *transition*.

N44 (VI.B.34) Jan-Summer 1933: Paris
188 pages ruled paper 21.1 x 13 cm.
First use: revision of FW Book III *transitions* (first set), II.2 early drafts.

Sheets II Summer 1933: Switzerland
Recycled matter from notebooks.
First use: II.2 early drafts.

N45 (VI.B.43) probably mid-late 1933: Switzerland, Paris.
136 pages graph paper 14.6 x 9.5 cm.
First use: random notes, only one unit used.

Raphael I late 1933: Paris.
Recycled matter: first batch of transcribed notebooks (probably VI.C.1-4).

Sheets III Summer-Winter 1933: Switzerland, Paris.
Recycled matter from notebooks.
First use: revision of FW Book III *transitions* (first set).

N46 (VI.B.36) early-late 1934: Paris, Belgium, Switzerland.
328 pages ruled, lined paper 18.9 x 12.5 cm.
First use: notes for revision of FW Book III *transitions*, II.2 for *transition*.

N47 (VI.B.40) Feb 1935-early 1936: Switzerland, Paris.
230 pages graph paper 21 x 13.5 cm.; some pages missing.
First use: revision of FW Book III *transitions* (second and third sets).

Sheets IV 1935: Paris.
Recycled matter from notebooks.
First use: additions to FW Book III *transitions* (second set).

Raphael II early 1935: Paris.
Recycled matter: second batch of transcribed notebooks (probably VI.C.5-10).

Sheets V early 1936: Paris.
Recycled matter from notebooks.
First use: late corrections to FW Book III *transitions* (third set).

N48 (VI.B.38) Spring-Sep 1936: Paris, Denmark.
200 pages ruled, lined paper 18.8 x 12.2 cm.
First use: late corrections to FW Book I *transitions*, II3§1 early drafts.

N49 (VI.B.39) Summer 1936: Denmark.
54 pages graph paper 10.5 x 6.8 cm.; some pages missing.
First use: random notes (none used).

N50 (VI.B.37) Sep-Dec 1936: Paris
238 pages graph paper 20.6 x 13 cm.; 2 pages missing.
First use: revision of FW II.3§1 for *transition*, II.3§2-4 drafts.

Raphael III 1936-early 1937: Paris.
Recycled matter: final batch of transcribed notebooks (probably VI.C.11-18).

N51 (VI.B.44) Spring-late August 1937: Paris, Zurich, Paris, Zurich.
192 pages graph paper 21 x 13 cm.
First use: revision of FW Books I and III galleys (first set).

N52 (VI.B.42) late August-early Dec 1937: Zurich, Paris
192 pages graph paper 20.5 x 13.2 cm.
First use: revision of FW Books I and III galleys (first set), and II.1, II.2 and II.3§1-3 for printer.

Sheets VI late 1937: Paris.
Recycled matter from notebooks.
First use: additions to FW Books I and III galleys (first set).

N53 (VI.B.46) early Dec 1937-Feb 1938: Paris.
142 pages unruled paper 20.4 x 14.2 cm.; 2 pages missing.
First use: revision of II.1, II.2 and II.3§1-3 for printer, II.3§5 drafts, II.3§4-5 for *transition*.

N54 (VI.B.45) Jan-Feb 1938: Paris, Zurich.
156 pages unruled, heavy paper 17.5 x 12 cm. The contents pages of Joyce's copy of *Moore's melodies* forms an appendix to this notebook.
First use: revision of II.3§4-5 for *transition*, Book I galleys (second set), and II.1-11.3§1 galleys.

N55 (VI.X.5) Mar-Aug 1938: Paris.
Missing notebook.

First use: FW Book IV early drafts, II.3§2-5 for printer, and II.3§6-7 drafts.

N56 (VI.B.41) late Aug-mid Oct 1938: Lausanne, Paris.
Final 206 pages of notebook VI.C.18; ruled, lined paper 20.9 x 13.3 cm.
First use: revision of FW II.3§6-7, II.4 and IV for printer, II.3§2-5 galleys, and Book III galleys (second set).

N57 (VI.B.47) Nov-Dec 1938: Paris.
100 pages graph paper 14.8 x 9.2 cm.
First use: drafts of FW Book IV§5 (finale), and revision of Book IV galleys.

N58 (VI.B.30) late Nov-late Dec 1938: Paris.
192 pages graph paper 14.6 x 9.2 cm.
First use: revision of FW II.3§6-7 and II.4 galleys, late corrections for Books III and IV.

N59 (VI.B.48) Summer-Fall 1939: Switzerland, Brittany, Paris.
96 pages graph paper 17 x 11 cm.
First use: random notetaking, *Finnegans wake* errata.

N60 (VIII.C.2) 1940: Vichy France, Switzerland.
148 pages unruled paper 11 x 6.6 cm.
Memorandum notebook: addresses, random notetaking, railway timetable.

Inversely, the Spielberg/Rose-O'Hanlon correspondence is as follows.

VI.B.1	—	N9	VI.B.11 — N6
VI.B.2	—	N5	VI.B.12 — N23
VI.B.3	—	N3	VI.B.13 — N20
VI.B.4	—	N33	VI.B.14 — N12
VI.B.5	—	N11	VI.B.15 — N25
VI.B.6	—	N8	VI.B.16 — N10
VI.B.7	—	N14	VI.B.17 — N22
VI.B.8	—	N18	VI.B.18 — N26
VI.B.9	—	N17	VI.B.19 — N19
VI.B.10	—	N1	VI.B.20 — N21

VI.B.21	—	N29	VI.B.31 — N42
VI.B.22	—	N30	VI.B.32 — N38
VI.B.23	—	N32	VI.B.33 — N41
VI.B.24	—	N35	VI.B.34 — N44
VI.B.25	—	N4	VI.B.35 — N43
VI.B.26	—	N31	VI.B.36 — N46
VI.B.27	—	N34	VI.B.37 — N50
VI.B.28	—	N37, N40	VI.B.38 — N48
VI.B.29	—	N36	VI.B.39 — N49
VI.B.30	—	N58	VI.B.40 — N47

VI.B.41	—	N56		VI.D.1	—	N16
VI.B.42	—	N52		VI.D.2	—	N15
VI.B.43	—	N45		VI.D.3	—	N13
VI.B.44	—	N51		VI.D.5	—	N24
VI.B.45	—	N54		VI.D.6	—	N28
VI.B.46	—	N53		VIII.C.2	—	N60
VI.B.47	—	N57				
VI.B.48	—	N59				

[VI.D.4 and VI.D.7 are *Ulysses* notebooks. VI.X.1-5 are not in Spielberg.]

From the above, and bearing in mind the minor overlapping (usually the result of Joyce going away and coming back) it is clear that *intellectually* the whole set of the notebooks comprises one long continuous allincluding diachronic integument, Joyce having paid no heed to the documents as documents in themselves. It is for this reason that the whole tale that this meta-diary relates remains for a total edition to tell.

II

Work in Progress

The Story of Finnegans Wake

4 Hieroglyphics: the evolution of the signs (I.2-5, 7-8; III.1-4)

> I have invented a whole system of my own — a great deal
> of it very childish — by which I keep my brains from
> falling about but I have been forced to drop most of it
> owing to the grotesque way I live now. I showed Mr
> Larbaud the signs I was using for my notes ⊓ HCE △
> Anna Livia ⊏ Shem ∧ Shaun. He laughed at them but it
> saves time.
>
> *(Letters I* 216)

In *The index manuscript* I wrote that "the translation of each
unit from notebook to draft was intermediated by referring
that unit to one of a small number of contextual invariants".
By this I meant that when Joyce interpolated a piece of text,
no matter how small, into his work in progress he invariably
did so knowing with which of his principal protagonists that
particular piece of text was to be tied. In this restricted sense,
the finished text of *Finnegans wake* is an extended inter-
phasing of spheres of influence: at any point one protagonist
is dominant. In III.3, the episode we call "Shaun-C" or
"Yawn", the situation is admittedly more complex. There,
the *voices* of different protagonists arise from the dormant
body of Shaun. So strong are these manifestations, they
periodically and ultimately fully eclipse the main character;
thus, at the episode's end, HCE is almost totally realized

and Shaun effaced. This interplay or inter-mutuomergence is a feature of *Finnegans wake*, but not a global one.[1] For the most part we deal with the protagonists serially: thus I.8 is almost exclusively concerned with Anna Livia, and so on.

Even before Joyce reached the point of inserting notebook units into protagonist-specific parts of his text in progress, he often pre-associated textual fragments *in the notebooks* with one or other of his cast of characters *even though the source-text is not otherwise distorted.* To put it plainly, Joyce frequently tagged a quote with the signature of the character in whose development he intended to use that quote. He effected this using a group of markers — curious little hieroglyphics of his own invention, the evolution and range of which shall form the substance of this chapter. Importantly, these hieroglyphics (the signs) only came into existence (and into use) *after* he had turned away from *Finn's hotel* and was working on *Finnegans wake* proper; they nowhere occur in the early, *FH* specific notebooks.

The earliest reference to the signs in the correspondence occurs in a letter to Harriet Weaver dated 24 March 1924, where he writes:

> In making notes I used signs for the chief characters. It may
> amuse you to see them so I shall write them on the back of
> this. I have been very busy revising over and over the proofs
> of the four old men Mamalujo. It comes out this week [in the

---

[1] ALP occasionally merges into Kate and into Issy, Shem and Shaun blend into each other to form a third character (unnamed in the text but whom we call Shem-Shaun), Shem-Shaun fuses with the Cad (HCE's adversary), and HCE dissolves into Shem and Shaun. This interpenetration of protagonists is rare and controlled, and is not random or eclectic.

Transatlantic review]. They now have taken a lamp out of
my room. Miss Beach was here. I showed her the room.
There is nothing to be said. Shaun is going to give me a very
great deal of trouble.

⊓	(Earwicker, HCE by moving letters {sic} around)
△	Anna Livia
⊂	Shem-Cain
∧	Shaun
⟨	Snake
P	S. Patrick
⊤	Tristan
⊥	Isolde
X	Mamalujo
□	This stands for the title but I do not wish to say it yet until the book has written more of itself

(*Letters I* 213)

Joyce also referred to the episodes themselves by these same
signs, so that we must distinguish carefully between their
use as episode titles and their use as protagonist indicators.
For example, in a letter dated 21 May 1926 he wrote: "I have
the book now fairly well planned out in my head. I am as yet
uncertain whether I shall start on the twilight games of ⊂, ∧
and ⊣ which will follow immediately after △ or do K's
orisons, to follow ∧d. But my mind is rather exhausted for
the moment" (*Letters I* 241). In this letter, the sign ∧ is
applied both to the character Shaun and, with "d" appended,
to the fourth chapter of Book III (the four episodes of this

part of *Finnegans wake* are designated, respectively, "∧a", "∧b", "∧c" and "∧d").[1]

Evolution

Using as basis the chronological sequence of the notebooks as detailed in the previous chapter, it is now possible to look closely at the development of Joyce's signs.[2] From an early period Joyce commonly abbreviated the names of his characters in his notes, rather than tediously and repeatedly spell them out. Thus, in the *Ulysses* notesheets we have "LB" for "Leopold Bloom", "SD" for "Stephen Dedalus" and "WS" for William Shakespeare. This practice of siglification

---

[1]   By way of aside, one will note that while it is very clear from the text that the first three of these episodes deal with Shaun, it is not at all so in the case of the fourth, in which Shaun hardly features. This puzzled me for a long time. In the first three of the episodes Shaun becomes progressively more abstracted from his central characterisation: beginning as Shaun in III.1, he becomes Jaun in III.2 and Yawn in III.3. III.4, on Joyce's word, is all about dawn ("I know that ∧d ought to be about roads, all about dawn and roads, and go along repeating that to myself all day as I stumble along the roads hoping it soon will dawn on me how to show up them roads so as everybody'll know as how roads etc" (*Letters I* 232, 29 August 1925)). The solution to the problem is plain (how could we have missed it?): the protagonists are Shaun, Jaun, Yawn, and *Dawn*: four versions of ∧!

[2]   Roland McHugh has written a short, still useful book on the signs (which he erroneously calls "sigla" — sigla are acronyms, as in "the sigla HCE") entitled *The sigla of Finnegans wake* (London, 1976). In this pioneering work written long before the compositional sequence of the notebooks had been established, McHugh focuses on the structure of *Finnegans wake* as published, and he argues that by using the "sigla" rather than conventional names (e.g., "△" rather than "Anna Livia") one can better comprehend the fluctuations of the narrative in which, famously, the characters change their names all the time. While I agree fully with McHugh, who has a deeper feel for the text than most commentators, I am here more concerned with a strict historico-critical examination of the signs.

was not, of course, particularly imaginative or innovative. In N1, the first of the notebooks used in the composition of *Finn's hotel* and *Finnegans wake*, one finds a small number of references to the printed text of *Ulysses* sprinkled throughout but, more importantly, many of the notes are associated with the characters and episodes of the earlier novel: "SD", "LB", "Pen", "Cyc", "Naus", "Hades" and so on. Significantly, these entries are *not* unused *Ulysses* material; they are new notes and all that the associations indicate is that Joyce had not yet come up with a plan for a new book. In subsequent notebooks, when he had at last invented new characters, these tags (which represent an attempt at presorting as yet unassimilated material) gradually evaporate, to be replaced first by "Trist", "Is", "Pop" and "Mop" (otherwise "Mum"), then by "HCE", "OM" and other initials until, finally, with Joyce fully out of *Ulysses* and *Finn's hotel* territories, he invented the signs, □ &c, which replace and serve a purpose similar to yet more abbreviated and graphic than the Homeric and subsequent correspondences.

N1 (VI.B.10)

This, the first of the long series of notebooks, was begun in late October 1922 and as such harks back to *Ulysses*. Thematically it is directionless. It consists in the main of bits of text taken by Joyce from journals and from daily newspapers of the time, particularly *The Irish Times* but also the *Daily Express, Daily Mail, Daily Sketch, Evening Standard, Illustrated Sunday Herald, Sunday Express* and *Sunday Times* (sources identified by Vincent Deane). One pre-eminently important cluster—detailing a street interview carried out by the *Daily Sketch* in connection with the once notorious Frederick Bywaters/Mrs Thompson murder trial — was destined, after Joyce had moved on from *Finn's hotel*, to become the "hoppingoffpoint" for *Finnegans wake*: the repercussions of the crime of HCE. To anyone familiar with the text of *Finnegans wake*, reading the newspaper's "Petition for Reprieve of Bywaters"[1] is a stunning *déjà vu* experience, and Deane can be credited with what must be the single most insightful exegetic discovery yet made. So important indeed is the deep-structure of the Bywaters case, Joyce used it a second time when in the children's section of *Finnegans wake* he had the children re-enact the crime. What is interesting also is the realization that Joyce had no immediate use for the notes at the time he copied them into the notebook; only much later did he fit them into his evolving scheme.

N2 (non-extant)

The second notebook, dating from early 1923 — the ur-notebook for *Finn's hotel* —, can be inferred as having existed but is not extant. Were it to resurface, it would be of the utmost importance and interest, and we would likely see in it an increasing focus on theme and protagonist.

N3 (VI.B.3)

The contents of the third notebook, dated March-July 1923 and as such compiled in the *Finn's hotel* period, splits into

[1] For example: "... Three soldiers were walking together in Fleet-street; one gave an opinion in which all concurred. It was the woman who was to blame. Bywaters played a bad part in the crime, but he was coerced. He proved himself a man afterwards ... A sailor, on the Embankment, was encouraged to speak by his fiancée, and said: I think the woman was more to blame than Bywaters, but I think there was someone else in it ..."

three categories. The first comprises extensive excerpts from
two studies of Irish history (revealing Joyce's concern at this
time), J.M. Flood's *Ireland: its saints and scholars* on
notebook pages 3-5, 8-12, 19-20, 22-27, 89, and 91-96, and
Benedict Fitzpatrick's *Ireland and the making of Britain* on
pages 155 and *passim*. A third source (discovered by Geert
Lernout) is Edouard Schuré, *Woman: the inspirer*, translated
by Fred Rothwell, on notebook pages 66-71 and 75-77 (this
last being primarily a study of Richard Wagner's love life).
Intermingled with these notes can be found a category of
notes featuring new fictional characters: the Isolde family
group.[1] These are generally tagged "I", "Is", "T" or "Trist"
as in the following: "Trist — Go away from me you — (she
goes) O come back" (p.1), "Is moustaches of beer" (16) and
"Trist — He — You? Is — (nods, nod, nods) 7 times" (61).
While obviously drawn from the legendary Isolde/Tristan/
Mark matrix (with Mark appearing in the notebook as "M"),
Joyce's versions of these characters are unheroic; "Is has a
dream, it is interpreted by Jung" (63) etc. In the notebook
Joyce is creating mostly comic and exaggerated, Nabokovian
situations and characteristics for his own notion of Isolde's
family and friends. She herself bears almost no resemblance
to the traditional Isolde, though in subsequently exploiting
the character Joyce re-integrates back into her persona
aspects of her illustrious namesake. The really innovative

[1]   Other notes are sigla-tagged: "SiD" (Simon Dedalus), "SD" (Stephen
Dedalus), "SP" (Saint Patrick), "LB" (Leopold Bloom) — including the
telling "The O'Gorman Mahon, When is a man not a man? (LB)" on p.30
— "JAJ" (James Augustine Joyce), "JSJ" (John Stanislaus Joyce) "BVM"
(Blessed Virgin Mary), "JFB" (John Francis Byrne), "TMH" (T.M.
Healy), "RW" (Richard Wagner), "SB" (Sylvia Beach), *inter alia*. The
abbreviations "H" (husband), and "W" (wife/woman), which reappear
throughout subsequent notebooks, are also used.

creation, however, is that of Isolde's parents. The father, originally simply that ("Is's father produces sounds from violin in bed", p.53; "Is father take Queen Elizabeth out to the people's garden in the park with a 6-chambered revolver & blow her bloody brains out", pp.18f.), coalesces into the more defined "Pop". The mother, Ma, or Mum, who is not yet clearly characterized, is "Mop". (Joyce, incidentally, seems to have derived the appellations Pop and Mop — ultimately to become the "two barreny old perishers" of Chapelizod — from a popular newspaper cartoon strip of the period.) The relationship is unambiguously attested to on p.61 in the first reference to "Pop" as a character: "Is's Pop & Mop (Pa & Ma)". Pop is a marvellously comic invention, as in "Pop gave wh. [whore] bob for job & 3d tip" (34) or "Pop made + [sign of cross] whenever saw éclair" (98). This characteristic, along with his escapade in the Phoenix park (exposing his backside to some soldiers while voyeuristically watching some maids urinating in what they thought was the privacy of some bushes), is ultimately carried over into *Finnegans wake* where it merges with the more sinister crime (a murder) of Bywaters.

A third category of material in N3 consists of notes concerning people from Joyce's own childhood; examples include "Alice Murray why nurse? Nurse Grier. Father Murray's brother. How much money did he have?" (31), and the intriguing "Hunter? (JSJ)" on p.36. These entries refer to a plan concocted a few months earlier when, on 21 December 1922, Joyce wrote to his aunt Josephine Murray:

> I have been trying to collect my notes as well as my poor sight will allow and I find several names of people connected with the family who were of the older generation when I

was a boy. I wonder if I sent you an exercise book with the
names of these persons at the tops of the pages would you
be kind enough (whenever you have a spare moment and
anything occurs to your mind) to scribble down in pencil or
pen anything noteworthy, details of dress, defects, hobbies,
appearance, manner of death, voice, where they lived, etc
just as you did for the questions I sent you about Major
Powell — in my book Major Tweedy, Mrs Bloom's father?
They all belong to a vanished world and most of them seem
to have been very curious types. I am in no hurry. You could
send me back the book in six months if you like but I would
feel greatly obliged if you could fill in any details for me as
you are the only one who is likely to know about them.

                                              (*Letters 1* 198)

In the event, he really was not in any hurry. He did not send
the copybook until 3 April 1923, at which time he was well
into N3. It is therefore probable that most of the "family"
notes in the first part of this notebook were repeated in the
copybook sent to Aunt Josephine. The remainder were
almost certainly reminders to ask his father for similar
information about people that *he* knew.

    In summary, N3 reveals Joyce's concerns with shaping
and casting *Finn's hotel* material. The Tristan and Isolde it
portrays are essentially the heroine and her beau as they
appear in that work. Her father, Pop, is sketched out, yet not
fleshed out. By the time he entered *Finn's hotel*, the name
"Pop" had been abandoned and replaced by "Earwicker". As
for Isolde's mother, she bears no significant resemblance to
Anna Livia, who is as yet unconceptualized. *Finnegans
wake* is as yet a long way off, though echoes can with
hindsight be detected in two notes: "wake story" on p.101

and "Setting—a wake?" on p.131. "Mum—letterwriter" on p.123 may or may not be a forecast. The brothers Shem and Shaun are as yet featureless and characterless; they do not yet exist, though "Is told stories to brothers" on p.128 does imply siblings. Chapelizod as a locale is also adumbrated, but this is almost predicated by the localization of Isolde's legend.[1]

N4 (VI.B.25)

The fourth notebook has come down to us in tatters: only 13 leaves are intact and the rest are fragmentary. In part compensation, many of the (unfortunately unused) notes from the torn pages were copied into SD1 in March 1931. It is therefore possible to reconstruct (at least in part) the missing portion of the notebook. A great variety of subjects are covered: notes taken from newspapers (such as the striking off of a Dublin solicitor with the unusual name of "Triston"), Welsh proverbs, details from a guidebook to Bognor and environs (in which, significantly, the name "Earwicker" first appears), words and phrases taken from *Moore's melodies* (destined for the "Tristan and Isolde" episode of *Finn's hotel*) and, toward the end of the notebook, liturgical detail intended for the embellishment of the already firstdrafted "Saint Kevin" episode (also for *Finn's hotel*). Kevin is here referred to as "Kev" and "Kevineen", "Isolde" is abbreviated to "Is" and "I", and Tristan to "Trist". Pop remains "Pop". The "Mum" in "Mum frees W from embarrassment (skin odours)" on p.94 refers not to Mop but to a brand of deodorant. Neither Pop nor Mop is an important

---

[1] The entry "Shem Cain △" entered upside down on p.168 bears no connection whatever with the notebook proper: it refers to later use and postdates both the compilation and early draft use of the material.

subject for (what remains of) this notebook. Chapelizod is mentioned only incidentally and, for the first time, Finn's Hotel, the "House that Finn Built" (p.82), is named, twice. We find a spattering of initials and sigla, "G" (God), "H" (husband), "A.G." (Arthur Guinness), "CSP" (Charles Stuart Parnell), but tellingly none of the signs ("∧c △" in red crayon on p.94 postdates the compilation and early draft use).

N5 (VI.B.2)

The next notebook in the 1923 sequence (dated August-September) is again a piece bag — from "stuffed chillies, boiled in rum" to "SP resuscitated dead" — requiring future research fully to explicate. It begins with a long index taken from a life of Saint Patrick and continues with many notes on Irish hagiographical and historical subjects. We find on pages 56-67 an extensive index deriving from a linguistic study, the first of many such in the notebooks, in this case Otto Jespersen's *Language: its nature, development and origin*. None of the signs are yet featured, and again we note Joyce's habit of using initials, including the anonymous "H" and "W" pair. Two striking new developments introduced in this notebook (and pertaining to the fifth and sixth of the episodes of *Finn's hotel*) are "HCE" and "O.M". Pop has essentially vanished, his role usurped by HCE whose character, if not fully fleshed out, is certainly under development: e.g., "HCE capable of any crime", "HCE hides in cave", "HCE drunk", "HCE at fire rubs hands think of beggar" and so on.[1]

---

[1] Pop pops up on p.62 in "Pop stammers" immediately after "Is hypnotised repeats French phrases learnt in childhood" and "Is's 1st words What ails wee Jock?". These are rather nice examples as, knowing the source, we can demonstrate Joyce's practice of appropriating the

The surname "Earwicker", incidentally, is sometimes spelled out: for example, "Earwicker mirror in closet-pan" (p.43).

HCE lacks as yet a defined consort — there is no female counterpart — though at points Joyce toys with a Biblical correspondence and a potential focus on Eve: "A-dam (Pa & Ma)" (13), "Eve f. [fucked] by ape" (14), "Earwicker (Adam) wakes & finds Eve" (31). The whole religious spectrum is within bounds and we find the extraordinary "T [Tristan] tries to kill Moses at an inn" (16) and the Christological "Stations of Earwicker" (31). Finn's hotel as metaphor is extended: "parl [parliament] in FH" (42), "Flying House (F.H.)" (94), the prophetic "Boat stopped by weir (F.H.)" (157) and the intriguing "FH W[omen] talk from various stages (the centuries) children play in courtyard. It becomes barracks, hospital, museum" (92f). Elsewhere, Joyce seems to wish to exploit a possible Noah's ark association: "Tree = Ark = Temple = Cross" (14), "ark = museum" (15). Predominantly, though, N5 is the cradle of the moribund old men (OM) and their names, dispositions and associations (shingles, will [testament], decrepitude, senility, stammers, broken voices, drying-up urine, rectal temperature, will [volition] and understanding) are here well developed. Joyce graded these elements together to shape the masterful Mamalujo episode for *Finn's hotel*.

Finally, the notebook displays Joyce's continuing interest in contemporary crime first evidenced in N1. He clearly

words of others to his own use. The source in this instance is Jespersen's *Language* which reads: "[one finds] far more stammerers ... among boys and men than among girls and women" (p.146); "hypnotised persons can sometimes say whole sentences in a language which they do not know" (p.143); and, "[the infant] Carlyle ... after eleven months of taciturnity [exclaimed] 'What ails wee Jock?'" (p.145).

delighted in the dry humour of these reports: "further blows were struck ... there was invitation to go down a lane to fight but witness said he was above that sort of thing & wd meet challenge at proper time & place", for example, or "A station sergt. from Lad lane gave details of a visit he subsequently paid to scene of shooting & produced a bullet" (165). These are almost certainly taken *verbatim* from newspapers. There is no case for seeing in these notes (as, for instance, David Hayman does in his introduction to the Garland facsimile) an early version of the cad scene in *Finnegans wake* (that cad has yet, yet soon, to be) but there is every reason for seeing in them (and in similar notes from subsequent notebooks) the inspiration (and more than inspiration) for the encounter in the Park and its aftermath.

N6 (VI.B.11)

Joyce continued to cull excerpts from crime reports using this notebook, dating from September-November 1923. He used a great many of these in his work in progress: for example: "gate locked to keep Murray in", "break my head, then break the gate on his head", "give him his blood to drink", "long list containing abusive names", "mission was on & he thought it wd reform her" and "kept abusing him from 10.30 a.m. till pm. no lunch interval" (165). Once again I should stress that these are not Joyce's compositions; they are the pen-products of, almost certainly, long-dead local journalists. If they look as like it as damn it to Joyce's *ipsissima verba*, it is because he imported them wholesale into his text and made them his own.

The notebook continues to include Tristan and Isolde material: "Is shit on by bird" (29), "Red Riding Hood (Is)"

(39), etc. Tristan is a guest from *Finn's hotel* (he does not feature as a significant character in *Finnegans wake*) and Isolde (who does) is well on the way to becoming a Lolita type. HCE continues to dominate as a referent: "HCE in kilts" (142), "HCE blushes — loves sins he confesses" (128), "HCE astonished to hear his fame" (162), "HCE cd remain awake 17 hours" (82). Also present are Kevin, SP (S. Patrick), B.V.M (Blessed Virgin Mary), H.G (Holy Ghost), Czd (Chapelizod), L.B (e.g. "Poor humanity (1 b)") and S.D. While the notebook consists of quite thick a jumble of heterogenous material, a few curiosities immediately catch the attention. A single use of "O Wom" (p.34) does not, unfortunately, herald a female counterpart for "OM" (who anyhow are androgynous). King Roderic O'Conor makes a rare appearance, sitting down and, like Giltrap's dog, uttering an unspecified monologue in Irish. HCE's mausoleum begins to take shape on p.128. More significantly, many of the coming protagonists (we are now entering *Finnegans wake* territory) make their entrances: the balladeer-to-be Hosty (48, 138), down-at-heels Festy King (49), city scavenger Kate Strong (145), Sickerson (93), Peter Cloran (79), the inimitable American hoboes Treacle Tom and Frisky Shorty (5, 113), and the sinister Cad (118: "cad's clothes too big for him"). Unique however is the first use of the signs: △ in a single instance "△ whistles" — and this, dear reader, is ALP's inception if one is not amiss, as I suspect one might be, in assuming that the triangle does refer to her (she is elsewhere absent from the notebook) — on p.2; and ⊥, also in a single instance (which may well have been added later): "comedy mirrors ⊥ mirror of mirror" on 105). Shem seems also to figure, just once, in "writer's cramp ⌐" (88), though, as noted above, there are also "SD" notes (in later notebooks

SD is subsumed into ⊏). In a nutshell, and even though the single instances of △, ⊏, and ⊥ are too ambiguous directly to associate with the characters ALP, Shem and Issy, N6 stands at the threshold of the crystallizing *Finnegans wake*.

N7(non-extant), N8 (VI.B.6)

These two notebooks span the months December 1923-February 1924. N7 was not posited by Spielberg and, except for perhaps a single leaf, is not extant. (It can be demonstrated to have existed by a careful notebook-draft analysis.) It should seem that the translation of HCE into the greater abstraction ⊓ and the creation of a consort, △, date from this notebook. It must be recalled also that at this period Joyce had moved away from his earlier notions for *Finn's hotel* (having essentially finished the projected sketches) and was concerned with the huge co(s)mic expansion of Earwicker (born in *Finn's hotel*) that was to result in *Finnegans wake*. The title "Finn's hotel" was, however, carried over into the new work and was not abandoned until several years later by which time — as boat, building and babblehouse — it had become absorbed into the work almost as if it were a living protagonist itself. For this reason, one is not surprised by the continuation of "FH" tagged notes in N8: e.g., "all tongues in F.H. tower of babel" (102) and "△ begin commonplace, introduce Finn's Hotel" (107). In the opening episode of *Finnegans wake*, written in 1926 after the basic structure of the new book had been worked out, Joyce describes the secret replacement/absorption itself: the book of Finn subsumed into the book of Earwicker.

The impish ⊓ and his somewhat more serious partner △

(otherwise HCE and ALP) spring into life without visible gestation in N8 (as said before, they were probably conceived in N7). The few odd written-on pages at the start (pages 5-31 of the notebook are blank) contain a number of sign-tagged notes: "△'s drawers" (3), "⊓ △ beckons to girls" (4). Beginning again at page 32, the first sign we meet is an S-like snake-pictograph set in opposition to a cross on p.33, presumably to indicate the devil-angel dark-light contrast that will so much concern Joyce in the coming years. On p.59 it recurs in "ʃ's skin = tatoo or syph". Later (but not in this notebook) this sign mysteriously becomes associated with Sigurdsen, the aged handyman in Earwicker's tavern. On p.34 Anna Livia is named: "Anna Liffey's red hair used for fire". A few pages on we read "△ in wig & blue specs" (37). The alpine triangle is used on subsequent pages in a string of characterizations: for example, "△ talks to herself" (94), "△ twinkletoes" (100), "△ source, bed, mouth, rapids, underground & out" (128), "△ has 111 children [has] 3 [children]" (189), and there can be no doubt but that Anna Liffey and △ are one and the same. ⊓ is equally manifestly the HCE character of the earlier notebooks. Unchanged are H, W, T/Trist/Tristan and I/Is/Issy, S. Pat and Kevin.

A curiosity arises however, assuming the filiality, with the newly emergent notion of HCE's son(s). "Shem" appears partly as a biblical referent but decidedly also as a potential protagonist: "Shem cuts old books, tables des matières [at] end" (95). Along with Shem we find other Genesis associations in extension of the earlier HCE-Adam, HCE-Noah linkages: Cain (who is cited by name): "cannibal Cain" (102) and "Cain has 1st navel" (109), Abel *qua* Abel, and Lamech. It is in this context that we first encounter the signs

Γ and Λ. They appear in a list of signs (the first such) entered by Joyce on p.101:

ΓΓ Δ T I ς Γ Λ.

With hindsight (and from Joyce's letters) we know that Γ and Λ designate Shem and Shaun, but the equivalence is not here clear. From the context, what is clear is that we have here the cast from the Garden of Eden. The presence of Tristan and Isolde can be explained if we assume that they represent HCE and ALP before the Fall (note Isolde's proximity to the snake). The signs Γ and Λ here represent Cain and Abel.[1] In the pages following the list, Γ is used extensively to designate Cain as Cain. Joyce was evidently reading at the time a commentary on Genesis that went beyond the biblical text itself. Thus, the otherwise inexplicable units "Γ lived 7 generations and was then killed", "Lamech kills Γ" (111) and "Γ led about blind, killed with boy by Lamech hunting" (113) can be accounted for as the (as yet unidentified) commentator's identification of Cain with the victim referred to in Lamech's rhyme: "I have slain a man to my wounding, and a young man to my hurt. If Cain shall be avenged sevenfold, truly Lamech seventy and sevenfold" (*Gen* 4, 23-24). An Earwicker-Cain relationship (whether or not father/son) is strongly suggested in the comic picture "ΓΓ comes out from Γ's wedding to beg at churchdoor, he wasn't what he was" (101). On p.115 we find "Γ refuses to sacrifice SD" and "Γ incest Byron & SD", the first intimation of the later extension of the use of the sign for the *Wake* character "Shem" (it should be recalled that the compilation of this

[1] This, incidentally, also accounts for their shape, a stylized C and A. I am grateful to Vincent Deane for this insight, so obvious in retrospect.

notebook coincided with the drafting of I.7). "Shem [not □]
jots down notes for △" (117), however, shows that the
extension was not effected immediately.

Apart from its appearance in the above list, "∧" does not
feature in the notebook (there is as yet no place for him in the
work in progress), although "Abel" does: "Abel butcher"
(110). The prelapsarian paradise scene is extended to △ (the
mother of us all), clearly an Eve figure: "△ gives names to
persons, ⊓ [to] things & animals" (113), "△'s youth in
paradise, snake A Satan B, where ignorance was bliss (Eden
Erin)" (115).

Finally, two other important themes make their debut in
this notebook: the slant-eyed hen, Biddy Doran (102), and
the status of HCE's marriage: "were ⊓ & △ married" (114).
Were Adam and Eve married?

— AN INTERRUPTION —
Check and slow back

What have you learned in the hills about ⊓, △, ⊏, ∧, ⊤, ⊥
⊣ ⊢ ○ ○ etc?

(*Letters I* 242)

Before proceeding with our survey of the notebooks and
looking into N9(VI.B.1), we can sensibly turn aside and
consider what Joyce has done so far (it is now February
1924) with the notebooks already reviewed. What exactly
has he written to date using all of this gathered material and
what narrative line(s) has he been pursuing?

By 1924 the original *Finn's hotel* with its distinct windows
or vignettes had been supplanted by a new novel dealing

primarily with the (original) sin in the park of H.C Earwicker, a crime in which he is implicated as both victim and perpetrator, and the public and private response to the allegations and attendant gossip. In preparation for the drafting of (what is now) part III but what at the time was intended as a development of the new character Shaun (who does not feature in the work undertaken in 1923) Joyce rather conveniently listed on page 163 of N9 *all* of the episodes of the new post *Finn's hotel* work that he had completed thus far. (It must be remembered that these episodes together form one long continuous narrative drafted in a relatively brief span of time, October 1923-February 1924, in what must be one of Joyce's most sustained periods of creative outflowing.) In the list that follows, note that the first and sixth episodes (I.1 and I.6) of *Finnegans wake* (conceived as afterthoughts by Joyce in 1926 and 1927 respectively) are necessarily absent.

> Anna Livia
> Cain
> Shem (where hvorledes)
> Collaborat[ion] on MS
> Hen finds Boston Letter
> △ writes petition
> ? is ⊓
> the Kings
> the Attack
> the Coffin
> Batter at Gate
> plebiscite
> train dialogue
> Sunday evg Bognor (cad)

Hosty's ballad
lodginghouse
lodginghouse {sic}
races
sodality
cad in park
Sin
⊓ riches
origin of name

Looking closely at these provisional titles, but beginning at the end and working backwards, one appreciates at once just how comprehensively they schematize the narrative that Joyce had already written.[1] In the paragraphs following I expand upon the titles to show this.

(1)   origin of name — ⊓ riches — Sin

These themes encapsulate what is now *Finnegans wake* Part I Episode 2 Section 1 (I.2§1) drafted in August-September 1923. This was Joyce's nucleus, taken intact from *Finn's hotel*. Here Joyce describes (a) how the King conferred on

[1]   Joyce evidently had at this point a plan in mind for continuing by reusing notions already in place in the text. He explained this a few months later in a letter dated 24 May 1924 to Harriet Weaver: "I am sorry I could not face the copying out of Shawn which is a description of a postman travelling backwards in the night through the events already narrated. It is written in the form of a *via crucis* of 14 stations but in reality it is only a barrel rolling down the Liffey". The list in N9 was intended to facilitate the structuring of "Shawn" (the protoversion of the originally unseparated III.1 and III.2). As it happened, Joyce did use the plan of Shaun's various "stations" (Shaun of the Cross), but he abandoned as unworkable the notion of the episode traversing in reverse order (as in the N9 list) the "events already narrated".

our stalwart innkeeper *cum* earwig-trapper the name "Earwicker" (one wonders in vain what was his earlier name); (b) his opulence and high social status; and (c), the degrading scene in the park where in the view of three soldiers he (allegedly) exposed himself to the gaze of two pissing maidens (assuming they were).

In writing this, Joyce combined elements from notebooks N1 through N5.

(2)   cad in park — sodality — races — lodginghouse

This next section (I.2§2), dating from October 1923, postdates *Finn's hotel* and is in a sense the "real" starting-point of *Finnegans wake*. Narrated here is a chance encounter in the Phoenix Park between a hair-trigger paranoid HCE and a "cad with a pipe". The cad, speaking in his native Irish, politely asks him how he is today, my good man, and asks would he have the right time. Earwicker, the self-declared victim of a campaign of vilification (see previous block), interprets the cad's remarks as a serious threat to kill or maim him[1] and responds instinctively and fearfully by protesting his innocence. The cad, thinking the man mad, departs, scratching his head. There is no actual violence. That same evening after his supper the cad tells his wife about the odd chap in the park. After sodality the following day she informs a priest about him and he, the priest, is subsequently overheard at a race meeting by two tramps, Frisky Shorty and Treacle Tom, relating the story to a school-teacher. Treacle Tom repeats the substance of the harrowing tale during an alcohol-

---

[1] During the troubles in Ireland in the early 1920s, this seemingly innocuous greeting was sometimes employed by assassins to distract their prospective victims.

induced slumber in a dosshouse bed in the hearing of three
fellow bumpkins (who share a common bunk), Peter Cloran
(a discharged drapery executive), O'Donnell (a vagrant ex-
secretary) and Hosty (a suicidal street-singer). Rising early
the following morning, the unemployed trio traipse into a
public house where their little group is swelled by two
"decent sorts" and in the course of several drinks (paid for by
one of the decent sorts) Hosty composes a mocking ballad on
the theme of Earwicker's exposure. Soon after, the ballad is
printed and copies find their way down every second lane in
Ireland: the scandal cannot be contained.

In writing this section Joyce combined elements from
notebooks N1, N3, N5 and N6.

(3)   Hosty's ballad

The *verbatim* text of Hosty's ballad (with music) comprises
the short section I.2§3.

(4)   Sunday evg [evening] Bognor — train dialogue —
       plebiscite

Having completed the composition of Hosty's ballad, Joyce
(in I.3§1) describes the destinies of the different parties
involved in the spreading of the scandal. Interestingly, no
mention is made of the central figure of the Cad himself in
the first draft, although this is rectified in the immediate
revise (I.3§1.1). We learn how one Sunday evening in
South-east England (Bognor evidently) an unidentified
individual "with already an inclination to baldness" (how
time alters appearances!) emotionally and evocatively related
to three schoolchildren a version of that fateful encounter in

the Phoenix park. Solemnly, we are told, he sketched for his youthful listeners the tragic scene: the pale fire of the moon, the monument starkly erect, the still trees, the gloved and pointed Earwickerean hand (that had killed its man). The very words of the "doomed liberator's" plea in self-defence are repeated. One of the children, it is said, never forgot the vividness of that afternoon recollection and years later recalled it to a cousin of "the late archdeacon Coppinger" while they were travelling together on a train. Returning to the present, the section ends with a plebiscite, a street interview concerning Earwicker's guilt or innocence, and an enumeration of the exonerating and mitigating factors that might have forced his hand (or other extremity).

For this section, first written in November 1923, Joyce combined elements from notebooks N4, N6, and, dominantly, N1.

(5)   Batter[y] at Gate

This title refers to the second section of I.3 (I.3§2), which Joyce drafted in November 1923. This details a banging at a gate or door, involving an attempt at forced entry and subsequent gunplay, although it might have been no more sinister than a case of a chance passer-by hammering a bottle of stout against a pillar in an attempt to open it. This section was followed immediately by I.3§3, a description of the house to which the gate is attached, detailing an incident in the house in which a paying guest (a German) was locked out by the owner (Earwicker) after he (the guest) had found that a not inconsiderable sum of money had been taken from his jacket pocket. The guest attempts to regain entrance, fails, and hurls abuse at Earwicker who is safely ensconced inside.

Eventually the German takes his leave, throwing a last few handfulls of pebbles at the bolted door.

The dominant source notebook for these sketches is N6.

(6)   the coffin — the Attack — the Kings

In I.4§1 (also written in that vigorously active November) Joyce focuses on the virtual prisoner left behind the locked doors of his guesthouse, which is now redescribed as a coffin or mausoleum. Earwicker's terror and confinement coalesce into an actual hibernation during which he feeds on his own fat. An account, meanwhile, is given by the official city scavenger of her finding of a series of footprints of an involved description near her filthdump at the dogpond in the Phoenix park. A vivid and confusing evocation ensues of the original makers of the footprints as they grappled with each other. The plan is involved and the identities of the two protagonists seem to blend somewhat, but it seems that the traces left behind them reveal that there a first man (the attacker, a heavily disguised HCE later named as Pat O'Donnell) with truly native pluck tackled a second man (the intruder, a masked burglar later identified as Festy King) whom he (the first man) evidently mistook for someone else. The attacker was wielding a long bar that he had and with which he usually broke up furniture; the intruder was simply walking home across the park while in possession of some stolen property. The pair struggled for a considerable time before the intruder said, *Let me go, Pat*. After further fierce struggle, the same man said, *Was six pounds fifteen taken from you some time ago?* There was still further mauling before a wooden affair in the shape of a revolver fell from the intruder who then became calm and wanted to know if his chance companion with the fender (Pat, with the long bar) had the change of a £10 note as, if so, he (King) would give him back the £6 odd taken from him the previous summer. The other (Pat) replied that he had no such a thing as the change of a tenner but he would give him (King) 4/7d to buy whiskey with. At the mention of whiskey the burglar (King) became friendly and went on his way with the 4/7d and a "hurlbat" (the revolver? Pat's long bar?) leaving the other man behind covered in blood. Pat, who bore up well under the onslaught, subsequently went to the nearest watchhouse and reported the incident. His health in general was good, although he was bleeding from the mouth, nose and ears and some of his hair had been pulled off his head.

The section ends with the subsequent arrest of Festy King who, when brought before the court and charged with both crimes (burglary, and assault and battery), pleads his innocence, claims it was a pig he had that he intended selling at a fair that ate part of the doorway and states that he clearly remembers the night in question: in the pitch darkness of that particular November night, he alleges, he "saw or heard unquestionably a man named Pat O'Donnell beat and murder another of the Kings, Simon". Finally, harking back again to the scene at the gate, he flatly denies throwing stick or stone.

In drafting this fascinating and intricate sketch Joyce combined elements predominantly from notebook N6.

(7)   ? is ⊓

This refers to section I.4§2, drafted in November-December 1923: the *Where is Earwicker?* or *Is Earwicker?* section. HCE has not resurfaced. Rumours proliferate as to his death and the whereabouts of his body. Local newspapers are consulted. Despite the rumours and the circumstantial evidence surrounding them, on the morning following the "suicidal murder" (see above block) a plume of smoke is seen to ascend from Earwicker's chimneypot, and in the evening lights are seen in a bedroom. Few, accordingly, could any longer seriously question the continuation of his legitimate existence. But who exactly is this "scourge of Lucalizod"? And what letter was it that lies behind the latter? (Note that Earwicker seems to live alone.)

Elements combined in this sketch derive predominantly from N1.

(8)   △ writes petition — Hen finds Boston Letter

These refer to I.5§1, drafted in December 1923 using principally the non-extant N7. In this, ALP's letter in defence of HCE is discussed and the various titles ascribed to it over the years are cited. The calligraphy of the original document is scrutinized. From this subject we turn to the issue of the letter from Boston (a letter *to*, it seems, and not *from* ALP), the semi-decomposed remains of which were recovered from the attentions of a hen by a child (Saint Kevin) on a mouldering compost heap; severe mutilation by the hen, alas, had caused further deterioration of the artefact. I.5§2—the text of ALP's petition—was drafted immediately afterwards but was then taken out of the narrative sequence by Joyce (he decided it didn't fit in) and laid aside, not to be reverted to until 1938 at which time he appended the *Finn's hotel* sketches to the ends of parts II and IV.[1]

---

[1]   At the time of its removal from the narrative sequence, Joyce intended to incorporate the letter into "Shaun", as is attested to in a letter to Harriet Weaver dated 15 March 1924: "On Monday I shall try to start Shaun the

Written in December, the letter derives predominantly from elements in N1 but includes also significant material from notebooks N4, N5, and N6.

(9)   Collaboration on MS

Although the identity of the writer(s) of the letter is considered in I.5§1, in I.5§3 — a very short section (later aborted) describing the zigzaggery of its delivery by the postman (originally Shawn) — Joyce specifies "the joint author" as "Iacopus Pennifera" and "Johannes Epistolophorus" (Shem the Penman and Shaun the Post). It ends with HCE's exasperation on learning of the letter's existence. The fourth and final section of I.5, written in the same period (December 1923-January 1924), analyses the letter (presumably a composite of the letters to and from ALP) palaeographically. We are told *inter alia* that it carries no signature, that the lines are mutually crosshatching and that it is stained with tea. The composition of the paper is considered. Finally, we are assured that the text is not merely "a riot of blots & blurs & bars & balls & hoops & wriggles": it is an avenue to reveal the "minds of the anticollaborators". Passing on from the sense of the words, the individual letters as graphic marks — the ees, the effs, the esses and so on — are discussed and, delving deeper, a characteristic quadrilateral punctuation (literally square holes puncturing the paper) is examined. After much scholarly debate and the realization that the punctuation marks coincide with the points of perforation

Post. This would make the second part of the book fairly complete with the letter" (*Letters III*). Note that Joyce here rather mystifyingly lumps together what are now parts I and III of the book and calls them part II. This plan was shortlived.

occasioned by the hen's beak, we are enlightened: the historio-
graphers have come to the conclusion that the *script* is the work
of the odious and insufficiently despised "Jim the Penman".

In drafting I.5§3 Joyce combined elements from N1; the
dominant notebook used in drafting I.5§4 is non-extant.

(10)   Shem (where hvorledes) — Cain

These refer to the bipartite I.7 which was written in January
1924. I.7§1 is a biography of "Cain-Ham (Shem)-Esau-Jim
the Penman" (Shemus is Irish for James): an anaemic and
repulsive black wino who survives by counterfeit and
plagiarism and is wellknown for violent abuse of self and
others. Also discussed are the mental defective's cowardice,
his addiction to drugs and his horrible smell; finally, the
hypochondriac "nigger's" retreat into a rat-infested cell in
the face of an existence unbearable to himself is detailed.
The section culminates in an account of his encounter on one
of his rare public appearances with a blond Norwegian
constable (Sigurdsen) who pointedly asks him, "Where
ladies have they that a dog meansort herring?", which is
doggerel Danish for "How are you today, my black
gentleman?" (*Hvorledes har De det i dag, min sorte herre?*).

For this section Joyce combined elements from N1, N3,
N4 and N8.

The second half of the portrait of the penman is an
apostrophe spoken by Shaun to Shem (as Cain) listing seven
improperia laid against him: a heresiarch, he is as sure as
Heaven going straight to Hell; sterile, he failed to engender
any progeny; a begrudger, he was ever a prophet of doom; a
layabout, he shirked a single honest day's work; a
murderer, he slew his brother and has been haunted ever

since; a malingerer, he lived out of charitable kitchens by wiping his eye and howling how he suffered; and finally, a mock artist, an unseen blusher in an obscene coalhole, it is to him, nevertheless, that "mummy", chattering ALP, is coming.

The dominant source notebook for this section is N6, but one also finds in it elements from N1, N3, and N8.

(11) Anna Livia

This, the last of the episodes drafted by the time of N9, brings to an end a special stage in the evolution of *Finnegans wake* (lacking as yet a dream, a Finnegan or a wake). Here Joyce describes the river/mother/protector ALP, otherwise Madame Earwicker, detailing her attempts to cheer up the doleful HCE, her musical and literary compositions, her (string of) former lovers, her present appearance and her Pandora's box of gifts.[1]

Notebook use in the first draft is mainly N8.

In summation and for ease of reference we can use Joyce's own list to indicate the rapid development of the proto-*Finnegans wake* and its dependence upon the notebooks.

Finnegans wake, Part One

Chapter One: not yet conceptualized

---

[1] Apropos of ALP, Joyce wrote (17 February 1924) "Anna Livia (Eve) means mother of all the living ... Dublin is built on the river Anna Liffey, (a stream only 50 miles long but with great windings, shallow, and darkred brown in colour (her hair))". The piece is cast as a chattering dialogue at twilight across the river by two washerwomen who as night falls become a tree and a stone.

Chapter Two
Section One: *Origin of name —* ⊓ *riches — Sin*:
    August/September 1923: N1 (dominant), N3, N4, N5
Section Two: *Cadinpark— Sodality— Races—Lodginghouse*:
    October 1923: N1, N3, N5, N6
Section Three: *Hosty's ballad*:
    October 1923

Chapter Three
Section One: *Sunday evening, Bognor (cad)—Train dialogue
    — Plebiscite*:
    November 1923: N1 (dominant), N4, N6
Section Two: *Battery at gate*:
    November 1923: N6

Chapter Four
Section One: *The coffin — The attack — The Kings*:
    November 1923: N6
Section Two: *? is* ⊓:
    November/December 1923: N1

Chapter Five
Sections One and Two: △ *writes petition — Hen finds
    Boston letter*:
    December 1923: N7 (dominant), N3, N4; and
    N1(dominant), N4, N5, N6, N7
Sections Three and Four: *Collaboration on MS*:
    December-January 1923/1924: N1

Chapter Six: not yet conceptualized

Chapter Seven
Section One: *Shem (where hvorledes)*:
    January 1924: N6 (dominant), N1, N3, N8
Section Two: *Cain*:
    January 1924: N1, N3, N4, N8

Chapter Eight:
    Anna Livia: February 1924: N8.

N9 (VI.B.1)

In early March 1924, when Joyce read *Anna Livia Plurabelle* to Valery Larbaud (the Frenchman was "enthusiastic" about it), the original idea for what was to become part III of his book — the delivery of the letter by Shaun the Post — was already in place. But he did not yet have a firm idea of how he was going to write it. While he thought about it, he tidied up the already-written I.8 and revised "Mamalujo" (which by this time had as he described it become "a sidepiece") for Ford Madox Ford's *Transatlantic review*. This period of reflection coincided with the compilation of the ninth notebook, which is dated late February-April 1924.

As might be expected, the notebook, sign-wise, primarily concerns the new protagonist $\wedge$ — Shaun (or Shawn), an Abel to Shem's Cain. As the notebook progresses, the ideas for the new episode gradually develop: "$\wedge$ has green paint for door" (28) "$\wedge$ plays bagpipes" (29), "$\wedge$ stations of $+$" (76), "$\wedge$ walks backwards" (76), "making a book $\wedge$" (90), "For $\wedge$ it is past, for reader [it is] present. We can't see actual present. $\wedge$ has lamp lantern — will o' the wisp" (160), "Stations of $+$, C blacker & blacker, $\wedge$ whiter & whiter", "$\wedge$ ray of light travelling backwards" (167) and so

on. These culminate in the reverse list of the part I
episodes found on p.163 (see the discussion in the previous section). By now, ∧ is certainly Shaun, the antipathetic
brother of Shem/Cain or ⊏, a nexus clear in such notes as "∧
city in Heaven, ⊏ — on E" (129) or "∧ natural ⊏ artifical"
(129). Shem, the subject of the already written I.7, is less
well represented, but is not neglected: e.g., "⊏ child prodigy"
(19), "⊏ A's [Abel's] caretaker" (49) and "⊏ reads future in
clouds, fire" (127). Thematically, also, the notebook illustrates the movement from Anna Livia to Shaun. An
important index deriving from Léon Metchnikoff's *La
civilisation et les grandes fleuves historiques* appears
quite early in the notebook (27 *et seq*).[1] Although he did use
a few units in his revision of the piece, this source arrived too
late to have any structural impact on *Anna Livia*. But
Metchnikoff's thesis of the river as the carrier of history
very likely gave Joyce the idea of Shaun carrying the
letter in a barrel floating down the Liffey. Also of interest
is an index — emphasizing the Chapelizod locale — derived
from Sheridan Le Fanu's *The house by the churchyard*
(62-64).

    Three innovations in this notebook are the almost total
replacement of "I" (for Isolde) by the sign ⊥, a neater
complement to ⊤; thus, "⊥ peak cap" (6), "⊥ shows knee"
(95), "low cunning ⊥" (118), "⊤ & ⊥ admire their photos"
(167); the creation of the sign ✕ to replace his earlier
"4M" (itself a replacement for "OM"), as in "Flood sung
by ✕" (76); and the creation of the sign ☐ to replace the
sigla FH (Finn's hotel), as in "competition for name of ☐"

---

[1]   For a commentary and transcription of this index see Ingeborg Landuyt
and Geert Lernout, "Joyce's sources: *Les grands fleuves historiques*",
Joyce studies annual 1995, forthcoming.

(66) (but note "plumber in F.H." on p.162). Otherwise, HCE and ALP-tagged notes abound, "⫪ appreciates gift of prick" (96) etc., including the important "delta = pubic △" (65) and the note that △ is a thief who has robbed her gifts (53).

Two curiosities are the emergence of a (subsequently rarely encountered) ALP-Is duality expressed by the sign △ and a fascinating use of ⟨ in the phrase "whimsical laws imposed on marriage bed w[ould] force a smile from the young & a blush — four presses & min. sleep to defy ⟨" (102), in which context it seems to denote the libido, that well-known prerogative of the Snake. Finally, two lists of signs entered by Joyce evince his concern with enumerating and controlling his growing family: a short "⫪ △ ⊏ ∧ T ⊥ X" on p.6 and an expanded "⫪ △ ⊏ ∧ T ⊥ ⟨ P ⋔ X" on p.127.

N10 (VI.B.16)

The next link in the chain — dating from April-May 1924 — is predictably and predominantly Shaun-oriented, with scores of notes taken from various sources on roads and roadmakers (especially Roman), transportation (from yoke to quadriga), the postal service (stamps, letterboxes, etc.), materials used as carriers in the conveyance of messages (tiles to paper, papyrus to pigeons) and other Shaun-centred themes. The text of a letter-in-a-bottle appears on p.72. Shaun as "Yawn" seems to be prefigured here (21, 26) as does a Shaun-Oliver Gogarty association ("∧claims £25,000 for hat OG", "∧ OG", pp. 94-96). Much less present, but not absent, is ⊏-Shem, *alias* Jem (77). Other, sporadic sign-tagged entries concern HCE, ALP, Issy, Tristan and, only rarely, the four old men (e.g. "✕ thunderclap" (25), "✕ play cards" (78)). The initials "H" and "W" appear once or twice, as does "SD", "Kevin" and "Papa". Ancient and Irish history are again to the fore and the notebook includes a dozen or so references to titles Joyce seems anxious to acquire (mainly on the history of Ireland). The only surprising element in the notebook (insofar as we are immediately concerned) is the unit "⊥ab & ⊓ no class" on p.84, which *may* demarcate the point of the beginning of the splitting up into a binary pair of the previously stable protagonist Issy. The issue of the siblings Shem/Shaun/Issy as young children together, however, is understandably as yet unexamined.

N11 (VI.B.5)

The not particularly distinctive eleventh notebook, compiled in mid May-end July 1924, reveals no significant innovation in Joyce's set of protagonists. Begun in Paris, interrupted by a stay (for an iridectomy) at Dr Borsch's eye-clinic (during which time he dictated notes to Nora, including the well-known "today 16 of June 1924 twenty years after. Will anybody remember this date" on p.37) and completed while on holiday in Brittany, the compilation of N11 coincided with the tidying-up of III.1-2 ("Shaun"), still regarded as a single episode. Joyce had run out of ideas. This accounts for the desultory nature of the contents, for most of which he had no immediate use.

Issy is well represented by the sign ⊥, generally appearing in counterpoint with ⊤. One unit — "⊥'s doll = Rain" (89) — is an early (though not the first; see N6: 51-55) reference to a doll, later to assume quite an important role in the delineation of her character. Despite this, the notion of the girl child is not otherwise pursued. Finn's hotel (still the name of the work in progress) remains stable as □ and as edifice: e.g., " □ temperance hotel" (1), " □ stocktaking, no dom. [domestic] pets" (64). The sigla "SD" appear once or twice, although one would have assumed that by now ⊏ fully embodies his persona, as in " ⊏ ½ blind speaks to a pillar" (127). Anna Livia is as usual tagged △ ("⊓ dreads scandal for △" on p.100, for example), but two notes (17, 92) use the initials "AL" ("AL {?handwriting}", "AL's look = a mute cry") which surely cannot stand for anything else. One wonders why Joyce regressed. The " K" associated notes are not overtly gender specific but definitely seem to involve not Kate Strong but rather Saint Kevin (as in " K chastity pure & simple" on p.101), much as Joyce still uses P for his counterpart, Patrick. ("K", potentially designating Kate, King or Kevin, repeatedly confuses.) Indeed, the importance to date of the characters Kate and Sigurdsen within the world of the diaries is minimal. The four old codgers, here exclusively designated by ✕, persist in their existence (" ✕ magi" on p.89) but are as yet assless. The unit " ∧⊏ grievance" (81) possibly prefigures the soon to appear ⌈.

Otherwise, in keeping with its directionless character, the notebook contains personal notes, a poem, and some few references to *A portrait of the artist as a young man* (which Joyce was correcting for Jonathan Cape at the time).

N12 (VI.B.14), N13 (VI.D.3, non-extant)

Begun in August 1924 in Brittany (whither he had gone in search of rest, recuperation and inspiration), the twelfth notebook shows a distinct tightening of focus, with its emphasis on Saint Patrick. Joyce evidently hoped that the

Irish apostle (supposedly born in Brittany) would show him
the way forward. On 16 August he wrote to Harriet Weaver:

> I have been thinking and thinking how and how and how
> and can I and can it — all about the fusion of two parts of
> the book — while my one bedazzled eye searched the sea
> like Cain – Shem – Tristan – Patrick from his lighthouse in
> Boulogne. I hope the solution will presently appear.
>
> (*Letters I* 220)

Unfortunately, some months were to pass before the solution
was to appear, and it would not emerge from the extensive
notes in N12 from books on Patrick and Brittany which in the
event turned out to be a blind alley.

A completely new sign, Λ, or Shem-Shaun, first appears
in this notebook. The two notes tied to the character are
unrevealing ("Λ you villain" on p.197 and "Λ bilingual" on
p.198) but the concept is definitely fixed. $\bigcirc$, the sign later to
be associated with the "twelve" (the customers at the bar),
is not indicated, I think, in its two possible appearances: "the
hunt (stones) O" (5) and "write O" (29). We shall have to
isolate the exact source for these elements before the
significance of the "O" is clear (elsewhere, and perhaps here,
Joyce employs "O" to mean "circle", "zero" or "nothing").
With the exception of ς and K, all the signs with which we are
already familiar appear somewhere or other throughout the
notebook: e.g., "$\sqsubset$ dogs bark at him to wash more frequently"
(222) and "$\triangle$'s children = trout" (176).

A few points of interest arise. "SD" continues to be used
almost alongside $\sqsubset$ and it may be that Joyce considered "SD"
notes more intimately referrable to himself than to Shem.
The curiously truncated form "AL" reappears ("$\perp$ shocked

by AL story") and its particular significance, if any, remains mysterious. The components of X are broken down in just one instance: "∧ to J that cough is no use to you" (200). In later notebooks, Joyce employs the sign X_4 for John (the fourth evangelist). N12 is also witness to the invention of the ass, their dragoman, which trails the four old men around the pages of *Finnegans wake*: "X totem (ass)" on p.140. Issy remains ⊥ but Joyce differentiates on occasion between the two Isoldes (Ireland, Brittany) associated with Tristan by labelling them ⊥ /⊥a or ⊥ /⊥₂ (as in "⊤ embracing ⊥ tells her of ⊏ & ⊥a" on p.216 and "⊥ whipped for ⊥₂" on p.232); this may explain the sense of ⊥ab as used in N10 (see above) as meaning "both Isoldes".

Finally, a short index on p.186 drawn from an odd book, *Psychic messages from Oscar Wilde*, edited by Hester Travers Smith (London: T. Werner Laurie, 1924) almost certainly gave Joyce the basic idea for III.3 or Yawn, which follows immediately the originally continuous Shaun chapter(s) III.1 and III.2. On 9 November 1924 he wrote to Harriet Weaver:

> I think that I have solved one — the first — of the problems presented by my book. In other words one of the partitions between two of the tunnelling parties seems to have given way.

He began drafting Yawn shortly after, in November-December 1924, around about the time he finished N12 and started on N13.

In Yawn, "voices" arising from the recumbent Shaun answer questions put to him in an extended interrogation by the four old men symmetrically crouched around him. In the *Psychic messages*, Mrs Travers Smith transcribes with commentary a series of conversations which took place in London in the summer of 1923 involving herself, "Mr V" (a reticent mathematician), "Johannes" (Mrs Travers Smith's spirit-control) and the discarnate spirit of the Irish playwright. The communications were effected firstly through automatic writing with Mrs T.S.'s hand resting on Mr V's (which held the pen) and, subsequently, by Mrs T.S. reacting alone with the aid of a "ouija" board. In both cases the communications were intermediated by "Johannes" who operated as a kind of spiritual switchboard. Having thus distilled the essence, as it were, Joyce proceeded (about a month and a half later) to dip into the text itself and he entered a much longer index (of which only the traces remain) from Travers Smith's book into N13. This second index formed the basis of a long passage near the end of Yawn where HCE takes on the guise of the whingeing, self-pitying spirit of Wilde. In one of his rare acknowledgements of his procedures, on 25 January 1925, just before he sent the fair copy to Lily Bollach to be typed, he wrote thus to Harriet Weaver:

> Miss Beach will send you a book of spirit talks with Oscar Wilde which will explain one page of it. He does not like *Ulysses*. Mrs Travers Smith, the 'dear lady' of the book, is a daughter of professor Dowden of Trinity College, Dublin.
>
> (*Letters I* 225)

N13, which dates from December 1924-February 1925, has not survived, although the Raphael notebooks VI.C.4 and VI.C.5 (p.220-end, beginning to p.91, respectively) carry a transcription of *unused* elements from the original. On the basis of these, and other than the *Psychic messages* index noted above,[1] we can detect no significant advance in Joyce's framework for *Finnegans wake*. The second half, indeed, regressively concerns itself with the "historical" Tristan, with notes tagged T, ⊥, M (for Mark) and K (for King). Of note, though, are the instances of $\perp_1$, $\perp_2$ (VI.C.5:25) and, anachronistically, "Mop" (VI.C.5:7). While the familiar signs X etc. are featured, Ⲗ is absent (but it should be remembered that we have only a partial copy) and, once again, SD notes appear alongside ⊏-tagged elements. A curiosity of the notebook is a list of key words (see VI.C.4:239) drawn from a draft of the HCE episode, I.2§1: "rootles", "cocker spaniels", "lady pack" and so on.[2] Finally, a note near the end of N13 (see VI.C.5:70) re-introduces (from "Mamalujo") the cabalistic *Finnegans wake* number 1132 in the perplexing note "C 1132 X".

N14 (VI.B.7), N15 (VI.D.2, non-extant)

The fourteenth and fifteenth notebooks were written consecutively in the period March-May 1925. At this time Joyce was creatively exhausted after the composition of "Yawn" (III.3), his eyes were in bad shape and, to top it all, he was preparing to move house. He did little or no basic

---

[1] Two small examples from this index rather aptly illustrate Joyce's characteristic technique of transplanting the words of others into his own through the medium of protagonist association: "adore ⊥" and "sociable leper ⊏" (VI.C.4:275) derive from the defunct Wilde: "That is better, but it is a little rustic. Still, I adore rustic people." (*PM* 7) and "My dear lady, do you realize that you are talking to a social leper?" (*PM* 12).

[2] In the case of the *Ulysses* notesheets, we find a similar self-digesting selection of words from the already written episodes of the Telemachiad. These self-quotations were primarily intended for re-inclusion in the self-reflexive "Circe" though, as it happened, most ended up as part of the tired prose of "Eumaeus".

composing, busying himself instead with tidying up some of the earlier pieces for publication in little magazines. It is therefore not surprising that N14 is barely legible and, to boot, scrappily compiled. Many pages are blank, others contain only one or two units. No new signs appear. ⌊, ⑀, K, and ✕, moreover, are absent. Of interest is Joyce's association of the historical Finn with Shem (76) rather than with Earwicker; the Earwicker/Finn/Finnegan dimension remains as yet unexplored. It should seem that Joyce was more or less floundering in the dark, again searching for a way forward. He turned to a study of the Norse origins of Dublin and entered into the notebook a long index from Haliday's *Scandinavian kingdom of Dublin.*

N15, which exists only in partial transcriptions (the notebook was accidentally copied twice) in VI.C.3 (pp.178-242) and VI.C.15 (pp.177-252), is notable chiefly for its Norse-centred contents, including a long continuation of the *Scandinavian kingdom* index from N14. Also of interest is another index (very similar to the one found in N13) taken from I.2§1.

N16 (VI.D.1, non-extant)

Compiled in May-June 1925, N16 (which exists only in a partial transcription found in VI.C.2:123-197) is not particularly enlightening. Staying at a hotel until his new flat was spruced up, the bleareyed Joyce did very little work. As regards our main concern — the signs — this notebook adds very little. The very few instances of "O" do not refer to the sign ○; indeed, in one case (VI.C.2:186, "⊓ sets O"), the symbol almost certainly stands for the Sun (elsewhere, Joyce uses the initial "E" for "the Earth": e.g., "bowels of E" on N17:131). Of interest is the re-appearance of $\perp_1$ and $\perp_2$ (VI.C.2: 174), the (temporary) creation of diminutive forms for Tristan and Isolde ("t and i children" at VI.C.2: 190), and the use of "$\times_4$" (VI.C.2: 180) to represent the fourth evangelist.

N17 (VI.B.9)

This notebook was compiled in June-July 1925, by which time Joyce, in his new flat, had got back into his stride. His concern at this time was in gathering material for the expansion of the Shem and Anna Livia episodes (I.7 and I.8). No new signs appear, though some amusing associations for existing ones do, such as "□ lunatic asylum" (102) and "⊓ female buttocks" (25). The *Wake* number recurs in "Ⅎ calls God to save him at 11.32" (19). K resurfaces, as in "his little babes (lice) K" (39), but remains ambiguous. In contrast, Kevin is elsewhere coded "S.K", as in "S.K prayer for rain" (1), in parallel to the use of "S.P" for Patrick, as in "SP baptises in △" (123). Vico makes an unexpected appearance in "pack [of playing-cards] reshuffle = Vico" (13), though the importance (greatly exaggerated) of Vico's philosophic system as a model for the structure of the narrative is not underscored. As to it (the unfolding narrative), an important note appears on p.19: "Part IV — dream of 1, 2, 3".[1] This does *not* (cannot) refer to the four-part structure of *Finnegans wake* (i.e., Books I, II, III and IV), as yet undetermined; it is rather Joyce's earliest idea for the fourth episode of "Shaun" (not yet begun) to follow after "Yawn". Like his original idea for Shaun (the events already narrated traversed in reverse

---

[1] Joyce perhaps had in mind something akin to the "Circe" chapter of *Ulysses*, in which the episode functions as the rest of the book dreaming about itself.

order), this one (to traverse Shaun a-b-c in a dream) never got past the first fence. As it happened, when eventually he came to write III.4 he cast it as a late-night copulatory performance by Earwicker and Anna Livia in the conjugal bed, as viewed and described *seriatim* by each of the four witnessing bedposts (the four old wakers X). A dream does feature in III.4 — one of the children wakes crying from a nightmare about the father (panther or phantom) and is comforted by the mother — but the episode in no manner reflects the preceding three. Finally, towards the end of the notebook (145), we find a reference containing the new code Λc, indicating "Yawn"; from here on Joyce simplifies his codes for the Shaun episodes: Λa, b, c, d now designate III.1, 2, 3, 4.

N18 (VI.B.8), N19 (VI.B.19)

In dating these two notebooks, two unusual chronological complications arise. Firstly, the early pages of N19 (the precise number is yet undetermined) were written in Paris in June or early July 1925, possibly contemporaneously with N17 (perhaps Joyce wanted to keep his notes for the expansion of I.7 and I.8 separate from his notes for the emerging III.4, ideas for which were only beginning to dawn on him). Secondly, when on 21 July 1925 he headed off for a long holiday in Normandy, he left aside (behind in Paris?) the incomplete N19 and started instead on a new notebook, N18. Only when this was complete (or nearly so) did he return to N19 and finish it.

N18, compiled in the period July-September 1925, reflects as it must Joyce's immediate concerns: gathering ideas for the fourth episode or "watch" of Shaun, and the further development of *Anna Livia* for publication. Regarding the former, we can be precise about dates. In a letter to Harriet Weaver dated 27 July 1925 he wrote that "While I was returning from an excursion to S. Valéry the idea for the last watch of Shaun came into my head" (*Letters I*, 229). The fishing port referred to, and its namesake (also near Fécamp), are mentioned on page 5 of N18: "S. Valery en Caux / – – sur Somme". Two pages earlier (N18:3) we read "$\wedge_4$ Dawn / Roadmaker", evidently his new idea. Unsurprisingly, therefore, much of the latter half of the notebook is given over enthusiastically to notes on roads, road-making, vehicles, and associated themes.[1]

With regard to I.8 ("Anna Livia Plurabelle") Joyce derived almost all of the later revisions (dated August-September 1925) for the third typescript and the galley proofs for the *Calendar of modern letters* from material in the first half of N18. One notes a particular interest in natural history, especially piscatorial: the two main protagonists, the man-mountain and his river-queen, are identified as species of fish: "salmon $\sqcap$ trout $\triangle$". One unusual source of esoteric detail dipped into is a little book by E.G. Boulanger entitled *Queer fish*.[2]

[1] Though Joyce famously described to Miss Weaver his difficulty in making III.4 "all about roads, all about dawn and roads", he never confessed to his failure in getting to grips with the roads part. I suggest that, despite the somewhat indulgent inclusion in the episode of a Prayer to the original road-builder (*FW* 576.18ff.), III.4 has little or nothing to do with roads. Joyce abandoned the plan, presumably finding it unworkable. Most of the notes regarding roads and roadmaking that entered *Finnegans wake* did so outside III.4, specifically in the two short passages *FW* 81.01-11 (in I.4) and *FW* 478.06-18 (in III.3).
[2] Richard Ellmann made an amusingly apt misinterpretation of this title when, in a footnote on page 123 of *Letters III*, he declared that "queer fish" was Joyce's description of his corrections for *Anna Livia*.

By the time he finished N18, Joyce had still not yet finally decided how to go about writing III.4, but a skeletal plan for the opening of the episode (which may however have been entered at a later date) is indicated (albeit cryptically) at the very end of N18:

$$\overline{\wedge d}$$

$$\sqcap \quad \triangle \quad \llcorner$$
$$\wedge \quad \wr \quad \dashv$$
$$\top \quad \bigcirc \quad \times \quad \bigcirc$$
$$\square$$

The first thing to note here is the inclusion of entirely new signs (and protagonists): $\bigcirc$, representing both the twelve jurors at the trial of HCE and, later, the customers in his bar, and $\bigcirc$, the rainbow or leapyear girls: "nine and twenty Leixlip yearlings". The protodraft for this, the last of the Shaun episodes (and a very zigzag affair it is indeed with its multiple subsections), opens with a perspective of the whole Porter (Earwicker) household asleep as seen through the eyes of the four old men. They comment among themselves on whom and what they see. Excitingly, the narrative is all relatively cast in the past. Shem, Shaun and Issy are *infants* and the parents are still sexually active. In the opening, the vignettes presented concern, respectively, Shem, Shaun, Issy, Saunderson (Sigurdsen), Kate Strong, the twelve members of the jury, the February/leapyear/rainbow girls, the old house itself, Mr Porter (HCE), and Mrs Porter. After this "night by night" continuous present tense overview, the four witnesses focus on immediate events in the household: the disturbance of the love-making partners in bed by the crying of a child and their subsequent actions. The episode ends (like *Ulysses*) with the pair back in bed, the man asleep snoring down on the back of his partner's neck, exhausted (after having done all he did), while she "the quean he cockufied blesses her bliss for to feel her funnyman's functions rumbling".

The casting of this piece was crucial to the evolution of *Finnegans wake* in that it enabled Joyce to progress (as he subsequently did) to the great themes associated with the protagonists not as adults but as school-children (in what is now Book II of *Finnegans wake*). Also, the series of vignettes at the beginning was to be replicated in much more detail in 1927 in a new episode (I.6) which Joyce interpolated into the already worked-out Book I.

N18 is interesting in other ways also. The important issue of the time of day of the episodes is partly explained in "Jewish nightwatches end of △ [episode I.8] 8 pm" and "Λ [start of III.1] midnight" (89). Elsewhere, the previously rarely seen character ⫟ is well represented; though, while he is definitely at times one binary character, as in "Janus ⫟" (124), in other cases Joyce seems to use the sign simply as an abbreviation for "Λ and ⫟", as in "⫟ sleep together" (138) and "⫟ Bros Grimm" (152). In point of fact N18 is extraordinarily rich in signs, including a whole family of nonce-signs, most of which are curious combinations of the basic ones. Thus, for example, we find the notes "⊠ all sing songs" (238), which probably means " X in □ all sing songs", " ▽ darby and Joan" (160) and other combinations, while ⊓ appears in various rotations and ʃ splits into enantiomorphs (mirror images, 146). Some entirely new signs appear, such as /\/\ meaning "mountains" (87), but these — like the aforementioned composite signs — are conceptually unimportant. At one point Joyce interprets his signs as pure pictographs, noting, for example, that ⊥ suggests a "girl lying on [a] causeway with one leg heavenward, lacing her shoe", while ⊤ suggests a "pastrycook carrying on his brainpan a mass of lovejelly" (144-5). Some of these fanciful images eventually found their way into *Finnegans wake*.

Turning now to N19 (VI.B.19), most of which was compiled in September-December 1925 when Joyce was actually working on the early drafts of III.4, what strikes the observant at once is, again, the diversity of sign-tagged elements (in keeping with the evolving all-inclusive plan for III.4) and the preponderance of related ideas, some of which were in the event left undeveloped: for example, "flour between beds ⊤, Ϻ & ⊥" (71), "∧ & ⊏ change beds" (91), "guard outside ☐ — new tenant not ⊓" (105) and "ape ⊥ ⊓ ⫙ descent of man" (156). Most of the crossed elements in the notebook were translated directly into the convolute protodrafts of III.4 — "✕ 4poster bed" (87), "⊏ dripping ink & methylated spirit" (203), "⊏ tears on pillow" (212), "∧ is blowing a bugle" (216) and so on, including Issy's new babyname of "Buttercup" (220) — but what is unique is the notebook's emphasis on the ⊏ /∧ /⊥ trio as infants or even as foetuses: "⫙ still in womb ⊥ waiting to be conceived" (215). With this notion of infancy and early childhood, Joyce has at last made a crucial breakthrough in shaping his novel. It is accordingly in pursuit of this new direction, and perhaps also wishing to put into place a "primal scene" to account for Shem's adult neuroses, that we find him making extensive use of material from some of Sigmund Freud's celebrated case histories as recounted in the third volume of his

Collected papers (London: Institute of Psychoanalysis, 1925).[1]

The first cluster of references (which begin on N19:17) derives appropriately enough from "Analysis of a Phobia in a Five-year-old Boy", an account of the treatment of "little Hans". Hans was suffering from several phobias including a fear of being bitten by a horse (which to the sex-obsessed Freud seemed "somehow to be connected with his having been frightened by a large penis" *CP* 165). Joyce associates Shem with little Hans; "little ⊏s" and "⊏ makes ⊓ nonno" (35-7, cf. *CP* 239: "The little Oedipus had found a happier solution than that prescribed by destiny. Instead of putting his father out of the way ... he made him a grandfather"). In the case of "The Wolf Man", Freud endeavoured to "explain" the patient's dream of a company of white wolves sitting in a tree and staring at him through a bedroom window. According to the good doctor (who I should say in passing excelled himself in *poshlost* with this particular "*détour* through the prehistoric period of childhood"), the gobble-you-up wolf was "merely a father surrogate" (cf. "vice father surrogate" N19:70) and the neurosis at issue, he contended, sprang ultimately from the patient having watched as an infant (necessarily through a brick wall, as later investigators contend) his parents copulate: "What sprang into activity that night out of the chaos of the dreamer's unconscious memory traces was the picture of a coitus between his parents, a coitus in circumstances which were not entirely

[1]   See in this context Daniel Ferrer, "The Freudful couchmare of Λd: Joyce's notes on Freud and the composition of chapter XVI of *Finnegans wake*", *James Joyce quarterly* 22-4 (Summer 1985), 367-382. Some material from adult-related cases identified by Wim van Mierlo and also from the same source (but not noted by Ferrer) appears in N17, e.g. the unit "⊓ female buttocks" earlier referred to.

usual and were especially favourable for observation" (*CP* 507). Quite patently, Freud's account of these cases gave Joyce many of his ideas for III.4, which opens with a child's nightmare about his father and centres on an act of copulation. In III.4, moreover, the highlighted coitus is ultimately viewed as a heavenly or cosmic event. This also is derived from Freud, "These dreams represented the coitus scene as an event taking place between heavenly bodies" (*CP* 566n.; N19:90).

Otherwise, N19 reveals a diminution in the number of now redundant protagonists: Saints Kevin and Patrick are absorbed into Shaun and Shem, respectively (92, 151). In contrast, the sign □, while still being used to signify an inn ("all come by roads to □", 191), is now enlarged to signify Anna Livia's letter ("Ↄ sets fire to □ by △ for ⊓⊓", 189) and by extension the book itself. Two years later, and perhaps contemporaneously with his abandonment of the title *Finn's hotel*, Joyce, circling the square, invented the new symbol ⊗, which replaced □ as the symbol for *Finnegans wake*.[1]

With N19 completed and III.4 ("Shaun-d" or "Dawn") under way, Joyce had created his full complement of characters in the manner and sequence described above. While the notebooks continued to serve him daily throughout the remaining years of his writing of *Finnegans wake*, our immediate concern to trace the evolution of the book's protagonists has now been satisfied. The remaining outstanding question can now be addressed: — In what order and when did Joyce conceive of the episodes that yet remained to be written, namely, I.1, I.6, all of part II and the concluding part IV.

[1] The sign ⊗ — a type of mandala — may have been suggested to Joyce by the coincidence of its parts: the circle representing the cyclicity of the whole work, and the cross its division into four parts.

5 Writing on: the triangle (II.2§8)

While the revision of the four "Shaun" episodes (III.1-4) in the spring and early summer of 1926 proved exhausting for Joyce,[1] it was nevertheless relatively straightforward work and so he was able simultaneously to begin to focus on a framework for a book that had to date, after all, extruded itself cellularly from episode to episode with no pre-existing ground-plan. With ten episodes behind him he was now in a position to consider the overall shape of *Finnegans wake*.

The first six episodes, ending with *Anna Livia* or △, were clearly distinct from the block of four "Shaun" episodes, and so both could be termed "parts" of the book in progress. But they were not to be contiguous: one other "part" was to intervene and another to follow. The first indication of his new plan is contained in a letter to Harriet Shaw Weaver dated 21 May 1926:

> I have the book now fairly well planned out in my head. I

---

[1] While engaged on this work, Joyce compiled N20 (VI.B.13), N21 (VI.B.20), N22 (VI.B.17), and began N23 (VI.B.12). Nearly all of the signs, in various juxtapositions, appear in these notebooks. Of special interest, beginning in N22, is the gradual replacement of "⊥" (Isolde) by "⊣" and/or (more rarely) "⊢". All of these essentially alternative forms occur in later notebooks, although "⊣" predominates. Also, the association of "ʃ" (formerly the snake) with the old Norwegian factotum Sigurdsen is confirmed by the unit "ʃ skald" (N22: 99).

am as yet uncertain whether I shall start on the twilight
games of ⊏, ∧ and ⊣ which will follow immediately after
△ or do Ϗ's orisons, to follow ∧d. But my mind is rather
exhausted for the moment.

(Letters 1 241)

As it fell out, he did not start on the twilight games (II.1) or
on Kevin's orisons (the first section of IV)[1] until, respectively,
1930 and 1938. It is notable, however, that the essential ideas
of these two episodes derive organically from aspects of
Shaun-d (III.4): children and dawn. (It should be recalled
that the notion of Shem, Shaun and Issy as children originated
in that episode.) A few weeks later, on 7 June, he sent the
complete plan for a quadripartite part II:

Between the close of △ at nightfall and ∧a there are three
or four other episodes, the children's games, night studies,
a scene in the "public", and a "lights out in the village".

(Letters 1 241)

Joyce's inadvertantly prophetic inability to count ("three or
four")[2] notwithstanding, the four episodes enumerated and
the idea for IV earlier referred to effectively complete a
structural plan for *Finnegans wake* which Joyce adhered to

[1]   In an unpublished article, Terence Killeen suggests that the "Ϗ" in
"Ϗ's orisons" might refer to Kate and not to Kevin. It is true that Kate does
feature, briefly, in IV§1, but the style and tone of the piece is Kevin's
(Shaun's).
[2]   The episodes as posited delineate II.1 (the children's games), II.2
(night studies), II.3 (scene in the public house) and II.4 (lights out in the
village). Much later, when Joyce was attempting to patch the *Finn's hotel*
stories onto *Finnegans wake* he was obliged to tack the "lights out" onto
the end of II.3 — thus reducing the four episodes to three — and create a
new II.4 (see Chapter 12 below).

for the following twelve years. It is notable that the *Finn's hotel* pieces are not included in this plan.[1]

Apart from the structure, of crucial importance in this plan is the idea of the book as a book of the night. Although already embryonic in Shaun (midnight to dawn), this is the earliest adumbration of a chronological succession of episodes filling in the hours of a single night. The idea possibly originates in a sarcastic comment of Stanislaus Joyce: on 19 April 1926, a few weeks before he presented his plan, Joyce (James) had written to Harriet Weaver, "My brother says that after having done the longest day in literature I am now conjuring up the darkest night" (*Letters III* 140). If we ignore the later interpolation of II.4 as published, then it is indeed clear that from the close of Anna Livia at nightfall to the dawnsong of Kevin following the cockcrow at the end of Shaun *Finnegans wake* does comply with this description. An insurmountable problem arises, however, with the first part of the book which was composed before Shaun or night had even been dreamt of. To adhere to the chronological sequence, part I ought to consist of a succession of episodes corresponding to the hours before nightfall of a single day. They do not. Days and nights and the following morning are inextricably mixed in them.

When he had finished revising "Shaun" (III.1-4), Joyce started to work on a section of the "night studies" (II.2) which he called "the triangle". Later on, when he revised the piece for publication in *Tales told of Shem and Shaun*, he renamed it "The muddest thick that was ever heard dump". He worked

[1]   Even so, when reminded by Harriet Weaver of the existence of the "Roderick O'Conor" sketch some months later, Joyce wrote that he would add it on to the end of part II (the "lights out" episode) with, however, the King's "last free supper" reinterpreted as a night out at the local.

rather quickly, entering notes specifically for the piece (which centres on the identification of an inverted geometrical figure with Anna Livia's pudendum) in N23 (VI.B.12) and N24 (the non-extant VI.D.5). Some of the N23 notes are clearly structural and pre-date the first draft: for example, "⊑ describe a circle", "∧ bisect a line", "⊑ does theorem for ∧", all from p.21, "⊣ reads album", "⊑ makes castle of mud, △ runs to it" and "∧ plays postman" from p.106. While N24 exists only in a partial transcription in VI.C.8-9, enough of the notes remain to evidence Joyce's interest in numerology and related themes pertinent to "the triangle". On VI.C.9:8, for example, we find an early instance of Shem's diagram illustrating the Euclid problem, replete with ALP-lettered vortices. N24 is interesting in other aspects also; for example, "⌇ Boots, cleans, peeps, listen" (VI.C.9:12) is an early identification of this character as the handyman around the hotel (his usual rôle) and as the policeman who listens and watches noiselessly on the road outside HCE's house in III.4. By 15 July he had completed the first draft:

> I have done a piece of the studies, ⊑ coaching ∧ how to do Euclid Bk I, 1. I will do a few more pieces, perhaps ⊣ picture-history from the family album and parts of ○ discussing ... *A Painful Case* and the ⊓-△ household etc.
>
>   (*Letters I* 242)

In truth, Joyce never did get around to writing these other pieces, which were probably intended to be included in the "studies" episode.[1] Instead, both during and following a holi-

---

[1] A year later, however, substituting Shaun for Issy and inserting the piece into part I, he did write a "picture-history from the family album" (see Chapter 7).

day in Belgium, he revised "the triangle" for Wyndham
Lewis, who had asked for something of Joyce's for his new
review. In the piece, Shem (Franky/Jerry/Dolph/Cain) not
only coaches Shaun (Kevvy/Abel) on how to describe an
equilateral triangle on a given straight line, but he also
initiates him into the "mysteries" of sex through a vision of
the mother's pubic hair. "The triangle" is a complex convolute
composition and Lewis chose not to publish it (at least not as
Joyce's work; see page 100 below). Just when his stout ship
was well under way, the sea began to get choppy for James
Joyce: his peers did not like his book.

6 *The prelude* (I.1)

The first body-blow was delivered in mid-September 1926 when the *Dial*, who had accepted it only the previous week (at a $\frac{1}{2}$d a word), rejected $\wedge$abcd. Feeling dispirited and uninspired, and for the moment finished with $\triangle$2 ("Mrs Delta", who will "babble anon"), Joyce then did a most extraordinary thing. Unprecedently for him, he wrote "to order". On the 24th he asked Harriet Weaver:

> Have you finished reading Patran and Tristpick and so on? A rather funny idea struck me that you might "order" a piece and I would do it. The gentlemen of the brush and hammer seem to have worked that way. Dear Sir. I should like an oil painting of Mr Tristan carving raw pork for Cornish countrymen or anicebust of Herr Ham contemplating his cold shoulder.
>
> *(Letters I 245)*

Before considering the issue of her "order", it is important to bear in mind that the subject of the short stories in *Finn's hotel*, which Miss Weaver physically retained, was brought up between them around this time (see, for example, *Letters I* 243). Evidently, innocently, she had asked Joyce what was the connection between his ongoing work and the 1923 suite. Hence Joyce's opening question. The timely reminder of the replaced book was immediately to come in uncommonly

handy, as we shall see. This aside, on 1 October Harriet
Weaver replied:

> Here then followeth my "order" ... Kindly supply the
> undersigned with one full length grave account of his
> esteemed Rhaggrick O'Hoggnor's Hogg Tomb as per photos
> enclosed ... There is a short monograph inside the church
> which says that the grave was reputed to be that of a hero
> king (of Scotland, or Northumbria) whose name I
> "misremember" but it began with O ... Such is my "order"
> for this book.

She enclosed photographs of a giant's grave located at Saint
Andrews in Penrith. Joyce was electrified: here exactly was
what he needed to give spin to his work in progress: the
notion of HCE as a (sleeping) giant interred in the landscape
and, beyond that, of a man assumed dead but sleeping. Even
better again, he now had the notion of resurrection to play
with and, with it, the notions of replacement of the old by the
new and cyclicity (Fin, again). He could even describe the
usurpation of Roderick O'Conor *et al* (from *Finn's hotel*) by
H.C. Earwicker with his wife and children in tow (in
Finnegans wake). Everything hung together on the fulcrum
of one word: *Finn*. And with MacCool came the ballad-hall
Tim Finnegan with his hod (who now makes his appearance
for the first time) and, with him, his half-erected wall (by
extension, the unfinished tower of Babel). With his fall off
the wall came the first Fall, Adam and Eve and all their
descendants down to Mr and Mrs Porter shagged out in their
bed. In a word, Miss Weaver's fortuitously brilliant idea
gave Joyce the notion for a chapter, or prelude, that was
destined to become the common picture of *Finnegans*

wake: a giant dreaming a dream of falls and walls, a babble of tongues, a tale of howes and graves and burrows and biers.

Miss Weaver's suggestion was doubly appropriate in that, on 22 September, two days before he wrote to her requesting the "order", Joyce had spent a day as a tourist visiting Waterloo. With a patch over his worse eye and his family in tow he had taken a bus from Brussels to the scene of the great battle. We know these details because the American writer Thomas Wolfe, our spy, was also on that bus, and he watched Joyce closely.[1] First they went into a little café to look at the battle souvenirs and to buy postcards. Then they walked up to the huge circular building on the inside wall of which is painted a panorama of the battle (done to commission by L. Dumoulin, a gentleman of the brush). Then they ascended the 226 steps of the *Butte du lion*, an artifical mound atop which is set an immense bronze lion (done to commission by John Cockerill, a gentleman of the hammer). A contemporary guidebook describes the scene:

> The loquacious guide discourses of the conflict, he directs our attention to the various points of historic interest, the positions occupied by the different regiments, the old windmill from which the approach of Blücher with the Prussians was first descried, to the great relief of Wellington and the dismay of Napoleon; then to the spot where the English stood in squares, firm and immovable, while company after company of the French dashed at

---

[1]   *Selected letters of Thomas Wolfe*, selected by Daniel George, edited by Elizabeth Nowell (London: Heinemann, 1969), pp.55-59.

them like billows on a boisterous sea ... There is no fee for
ascending the Mound, but a small gratuity (25 c.) is expected.[1]

Which is to say, a *tip* was expected. Joyce walked next to the
guide, asking him questions. Tip. On the way home in the
bus, he sat with the driver on the front seat, and asked a great
many more questions. Tip.

Spurred on by this serendipity, between the end of
September 1926 and the end of January 1927 Joyce prepared
the key notebook N25 (VI.B.15) in which the subject matters
of △2 and I.1 interface. N25 contains in seminal form almost
the whole of the prelude, from "⫟ at S Anne has fieldglasses
trained on ⊣" (p.22: this reappears as Earwicker-Wellington
spying through a telescope on the flanks of the two "jinnies")
to the first formulation of the book's original opening words,
a quasi-title "Howth Castle & Environs" (33). Notes appear
on the history of Howth Castle and its association with the St.
Lawrence family and Grace O'Malley (the "Prankquean" of
I.1); on the notion of a dead HCE ("foxes frightened by keen
for ⫟", p.40); on the conjunction of the protagonists in the
Willingdone/three lipoleums/two jinnies/me belchum (⫟ /
∧⊏⫧/ ⊣⊢ /ϟ) interaction (a recasting of the prototypal scene
in the park between HCE, the three soldiers and the two
maids, but now with old Joe looking on); on the date span
covered in the I.1 Annals ("566 BC to 566 AD" — 1132
years (65)); on the four old men, harking back to their
original appearance floating in the drink in the *Finn's hotel*
suite; on big-backsided Finn McCool, on ancient Egypt, on
the physiological effects of sleep; on the evolution of writing

[1] *The traveller's handbook for Belgium and the Ardennes* (London:
Thomas Cook, 1924), p.93.

(from Clodd's *The story of the alphabet*); and so on down
from the first formulation of the first of the famous
hundredlettered thunderwords that reverberate throughout
Finnegans wake (155: the first to sound is an agglutination
of the word for thunder in a medley of languages, translating
"thunderthunderthunderthunder...") to fragmentary scraps
for the dialogue passages and a listing of Norse gods, and so
on and so on in amazing proliferation. One particularly
significant note, "b [battle] of Clontarf symbol of night v
[versus] day" (205), reveals Joyce at work developing for the
first time the Brunonian idea of $\wedge$ / $\sqsubset$ light/dark, wake/sleep,
life/death, consciousness/unconsciousness — opposites in
conflict — with their respective interfacing in twilight, after-
life and subconsciousness that unifies his work with the
eschatology of the *Egyptian book of the dead* and provides
him with a pivotal historical moment (the expulsion of the
Danes from Ireland in 1014) that is repeatedly referred to in
Finnegans wake.

The prelude itself was written out in a sustained outflowing
of energy. Its several essentially distinct sections deal
respectively with: the hero as primal builder, as sacrificial
fish, as slumbering sea-monster and as a giant interred in the
landscape (I.1§1a); the retiring "gnarlybird" and her piece
bag (a version of ALP collecting her gifts) and (Viconian)
historical movement (I.1§1b); the war-scarred Dublin Annals
compiled over the centuries by the four Annalists (I.1§1c);
a version of the Edgar Quinet's flower-conceit in which
wildflowers, though delicate in themselves, survive
unchanged the fall of armies and empires to bloom anew
(I.1§1d); the prehistorical Jute-Mutt (Shem-Shaun) deaf-
mute dialogue on the aftermath of battle (Clontarf) and on
death as leveller (I.1§1e); the literature-centred history of

letters (I.1§2a); the riddle-posing and kidnapping of the
love-child by the mannish Prankquean; and, finally, the
attempts by the drunken revellers at the wake to dissuade the
dormant Finn from reviving (I.1§2b).

Joyce's excitement in the face of this new array of
forces is reflected in a letter of 8 November 1926 to Harriet
Weaver:

> I set to work at once on your esteemed order and so hard
> indeed that I almost stupefied myself and stopped ... I am
> putting the piece in place of honour, namely the first pages
> of the book. Will try to deliver same punctual by Xmas. But
> cd send sample, viz, page 1, if consumer so desires. The
> book really has no beginning or end. (Trade secret, registered
> at Stationers Hall.) It ends in the middle of a sentence and
> begins in the middle of the same sentence. Your piece is the
> prelude ... The third part you have also ∧abcd. I have
> written out only a small part of the second [part] ending
> with Roderick O'C. The fourth [part] will be shorter than
> the others.
>
> (*Letters I* 246)

He continued to work on the prelude for the next two months.
He finished it on 16 December, had it typed out and sent it
(the typescript), as a gift, to Miss Weaver. The selfsame
typescript was auctioned in 1976 by Christies but was
returned the following day by the purchaser, who described
it as a "notorious document" which members of the Weaver
family had allegedly been trying to sell for years.

In January 1927 Ezra Pound wrote that he was bringing
out a review, but he added that he did not want anything in
it from Joyce's work in progress; earlier, on 15 November

1926, he had said that he did not care for Shaun. The Shaun typescript has since disappeared.

Wyndham Lewis neither acknowledged nor returned "the triangle" typescript sent to him. He did, however, make use of it by incorporating fragments from it in his novel *The Childermass* which was published in June 1928. Murder willing itself out, the typescript of "the triangle" turned up fifty years later among Lewis's papers at Cornell University.

Bitterest of all to Joyce was Harriet Weaver's rejection of "the prelude". On 1 Feb 1927, in response to her lack of enthusiasm, he wrote morosely: "Your letter gave me a nice little attack of brainache. I conclude that you do not like the piece I did? I have been thinking over it. It is all right, I think — the best I could do" (*Letters I* 249).

7   *The questionnaire* (I.6)

A new figure entered into James Joyce's life in December 1926. This was Eugene Jolas, an American citizen of German/ French extraction who had spent his childhood in Lorraine. Jolas intended to set up in Paris a new review to be called *transition* and he approached Joyce for a contribution. Joyce was only too happy to oblige. An agreement was soon put in place whereby *transition* would print *seriatim* (at twenty francs a page) all of the episodes of the book so far written. This arrangement was destined to continue, with a few interruptions, until 1938.

On a personal level, Joyce soon became fast friends with Jolas and with his wife Maria. He was grateful for the American's response to his work in progress, though Jolas's enthusiasm had its limitations. While very intelligent, he was not of the intellectual calibre of Pound or Lewis. In addition, as a proponent of what he called the "Revolution of the word" Jolas was somewhat radical and liked the *Wake* for its very "unintelligibility". (In this he has been followed by too many recent commentators.) Joyce, like the cad, must surely have scratched his head. Still, it was the best offer available.

Joyce worked very hard through the spring and early summer of 1927 revising the episodes of part I for *transition*. At the same time, and in order to entice Miss Weaver back onto his team, so to speak, he played with her a kind of game,

sending her clues and asking her to try to guess the title of his
book. For the same purpose, he set in train an investigation
of Pound's "soundness of judgement", citing for the
prosecution the case of one Ralph Cheever Dunning, an inept
young poet that Pound had begun to champion. Also, he sent
her a copy of *The enemy*, Lewis's review, to read. By mid-
July, after he had finished revising I.5 (the investigation of
the letter), all these factors coalesced with other considerations
to inspire him to write a new chapter, which was to be his last
interpolation into part I. The first mention of the new episode
in the correspondence occurs in a letter to Harriet Weaver
dated 26 July 1927: "I am working night and day at a piece
I have to insert between the last [I.5] and [[I.7]" (*Letters
III* 163).

The new episode, I.6, which Joyce termed "the
questionnaire", was compelled for several reasons. Firstly,
he wanted to make sure that all of his characters (including
Shaun) were properly represented in part I (this was certainly
not the case up to 1926). Secondly, as mentioned earlier (see
page 85), he needed to balance the episode in part III where
all of the protagonists are conjured up by Yawn. Thirdly, he
wanted an opportunity to answer his critics (although, to a
degree, he had done this in his revision of I.5). In the piece,
twelve questions are posed (including Joyce's question to
Miss Weaver, What is the title?) and twelve answers are
given (including, in the pertinent answer, some of Miss
Weaver's guesses). As in III.3 ("Yawn"), while Shaun is the
ostensible answerer throughout, each question and answer
set is couched in the style and rhythm of the particular
protagonist involved. In his own question (the longest, as it
happens) Shaun appears as "Professor Jones", a thinly
disguised Wyndham Lewis.

The subjects of the individual questions are indicated by
signs on a page of the manuscript (BL Add.MS 47473-150v)
written immediately before the first draft. These are:-

1	⊓	[HCE]
2	△	[ALP]
3	□	[book title/pub name]
4	X	[the 4 old men]
5	⟨	[Sigurdsen, old Joe]
6	K	[the sweep, Kate Strong]
7	○	[the 12 customers]
8	◯	[the 29 leapyear girls]
9	[blank]	
10	⊣	[Issy]
11	∧	[Shaun]
12	⊏	[Shem]

This list is interesting in a number of ways and from the
manuscript text of the questions/answers we can associate
each sign with an identifiable protagonist. A second numbered
list of the signs was made soon after (MS 47473.132v,
apparently just before he came to draft the ninth question)
and is identical to the above except that Joyce now provides
the newly created sign ⊗ as referent for the ninth question
(which refers to the world-view of the creator of the book).[1]
In faircopying the piece, Joyce wrote the corresponding sign
in the margin beside each question, apparently intending that
they all be included in the published version. A point of

---

[1]   The creation and interaction of Joyce's signs reminds one of particle
creation, with quarks and gluons giving rise to protons and neutrons and
so on through the creative expansion of the original soup and the resultant
variety combining to form a universe.

interest in the faircopy is the use of $\langle$ and not $\rangle$ for question five, descriptive of "poor old Joe", the factotum round the inn. Also, Joyce surprisingly and regressively uses the old sign $\perp$ instead of $\dashv$ for the "Issy" question.

Looking into the notebooks, one finds that the dominant sourcebook for the first draft, N27, is missing. This is a great loss. The preceding notebook, however, N26(VI.B.18) — a very few units of which were transfered to the first draft — provides most of the material for the first revision. In this notebook, written in the period between March and July 1927, Kate Strong is coded both "KS" and "K", as in "KS tells story of □" (86) and "K Blackcullen's jam" (251). No example of $\perp$ appears, though both $\vdash$ and $\dashv$ can be found in conjunction: e.g., "$\dashv$ sends $\top$ to $\vdash$" (277). One unit may amalgamate both in a transitory sign: "$\top$ sells $\vdash\dashv$" (284). The notebook is otherwise notable for the relative frequency of ○ units, some of which are, to say the least, ambiguous: "□ puts ear to river = ○" (9) and "○ 3 dreams" (283). It is possible that these were early ideas for I.6 which is, after all, a twelvesome. Other cases are less cryptic: "○ alarm clock" (13), "monkeyglands renew ○ zoo" (67), or "12 + 1 = 13 ○" [the twelve jurors and their clerk] $4 + 1 = 5$ X" [the four and their ass]" (148). One rather curious entry reads "Finn asks ○ what then is love" (103), which is the leading question asked in the ○ environment of question eight.

I.6, with its strings of attributes, does not add anything to the narrative. Nor does it sit very comfortably where it is positioned, interrupting the natural progression of I.5 (the identification of the scribe as Shem) into I.7 (a description of Shem). For all that, it is marvellously entertaining and the occasion for the appearance — very late in the drafting — of the first of Joyce's incomparable fables, "The mookse and the gripes". With the interpolation of the fable, the scales tipped the other way and so, to balance *that*, in the following year Joyce was obliged to compose a second fable, "The ondt and the gracehoper" (also aimed at Lewis) for insertion into part III.

Finally, after he had finished the piece, Joyce with tongue in cheek admitted to Harriet Weaver to a desire (unrealized) to add a thirteenth question, Who is that infallible who pontificates over the arts of architecture, sculpture, drawing, painting, fiction, economics, philosophy etc etc etc etc, who writes as if he were the pope and preaches as if he were a parson?

8 transition & éditions de luxe

In the years between the autumn of 1927 and the early summer of 1930, Joyce devoted himself to "completing" the revision of all of those parts of *Finnegans wake* that he had already written. The revisions were in all cases significant (his texts expanded to double their original lengths); yet, other than the writing of the fable "The ondt and the gracehoper" in February 1928, he did no basic composing. In submitting the episodes *seriatim* to *transition*, he stuck to the sequential order as outlined in his 1926 plan: first part I (I.1-I.8), then what he had written of part II (II.2§8, the "Triangle" part of the "studies") and, finally, part III (III.1-4).[1] On 19 October 1929, while he was finishing correcting the proofs of III.4 ("Shaun-d") for *transition*, he wrote to Harriet Weaver: "I have finished however the work for *transition* and also my connection with the review as you will see by a note in it" (*Letters I* 285). It is important to note that he did not publish in *transition* either in this period or later (he resumed his connection with the review in 1932) any of the six episodes of the *Finn's hotel* suite that he had laid aside in 1924. They were not yet part of *Finnegans wake*.

In addition to the regular appearances of his work in progress in *transition*, Joyce around this time began to publish selected episodes in *éditions de luxe*. He chose

---

[1] For further details of these publications, see Appendix B.

pieces which he felt could stand on their own and which would be accessible to the general public. He began, reasonably enough, with *Anna Livia Plurabelle* (I.8), of which he was especially proud. This appeared in October 1928. The two fables and "the triangle" were next brought together (and again revised) for *Tales told of Shem and Shaun* (August 1929). Finally, after he had finished with *transition*, he worked on the closing section of III.3 which, very extensively expanded, appeared in April 1930 under the title *Haveth childers everywhere*. Of these three, the first two were critical successes, relatively speaking; the third was not. The reason for this is not any diminution of Joyce's powers (if anything, they had increased), rather it lies in the increasing corruption of his text. He had begun to lose control of its transmission into print.

In August 1928, Joyce's eyes deteriorated suddenly, and he had to abandon the work that he had only just begun (the revision of III.3 for *transition*). He could scarcely read a word and did little or no work until December, when a specially prepared typescript of the episode (extra-large print) was made. As even this aid did not suffice, he took to memorizing large swathes of the text so that he would know what was on which page when he came to revise it. The revision itself, which took about two months to complete, is extremely complex and comprehensive, so that it is not surprising that numerous serious errors appear in the *transition* version. The whole situation was worsened when, during this period, Nora became ill and was obliged to go into hospital for a hysterectomy. On 26 January 1929 Joyce wrote to his brother Stanislaus: "I return to the clinic with Nora on the fourth ... My reading sight seems to have come to an end ... with the help of about ten assistants I was able to check the

next installment for *transition* which comes out this week"
(*Letters III* 187). The "assistants", alas, were another cause
of error, as to a man (and to a woman) they did not understand
what it was that they were checking.

Joyce's eyes recovered sufficiently in the spring of 1929
to allow him to revise "the triangle" and the two fables for
Tales told without the necessity for a special typescript; the
published version is consequently free of any more textual
corruption than would be expected in the natural run of
things. By the autumn his sight deteriorated again and, in
order to prepare III.4 for *transition*, another special typescript
had to be made. By the spring of 1930 his eyes were
particularly bad, as an inspection of the manuscripts concerned
in the revision of *Haveth childers everywhere* amply
illustrates. For this episode, not only was the base text (pages
taken from the *transition* publication) already appallingly
corrupt, but the auxesis — the total set of additions (once
again complex and extensive) — is literally all over the place
and in the handwriting of five or six different people (Stuart
Gilbert, Helen Fleischmann, the Colums and a new recruit
named Paul Léon), with only a small part in Joyce's
blindman's scrawl. What is astonishing is not that the text as
published is hopelessly corrupt, which it is, but that the
corruption — although with great difficulty — can be
reversed and the errors removed.

When this is done, and it is no easy task, *Haveth childers
everywhere* is transformed and becomes precisely what
Joyce intended it to be: a fitting consort for *Anna Livia
Plurabelle*, lyrical, freeflowing and immeasurably moving.
HCE's defence of his life, pathetic at first, gathers momentum
until, at the end, it becomes utterly convincing. In the midst
of blindness, working on a totally inadequate text, James

Joyce somehow managed (in what astral plane?) to write a masterpiece, though it did not come out so on the paper. I realise, of course, that the reader will have to take my word for this, for the present at least, until the critical edition of *Finnegans wake* is made available.

As can be ascertained from the chronological listing in Chapter 3, notebooks N28 to N35 (first half) were used for the revision for *transition* and for the first two of the *éditions de luxe*, while N35 (second half) to N37 were compiled specially for *Haveth childers everywhere*. While the notebooks illustrate Joyce's interests at the time (the author of *Alice in wonderland*, the *Book of the dead*, the Papacy, the Eastern Church, etc etc etc),[1] they contain no significant structural notes or any new or altered protagonists.

[1] A comprehensive account of the period must, of course, await a fully annotated edition of the notebooks concerned. For a brief outline of the growth of *Haveth childers everywhere* and for a list of the sources used, see the Appendix to Danis Rose and John O'Hanlon, *Understanding Finnegans wake* (1982).

9 Children's games (II.1)

After he had completed *Haveth childers everywhere*, Joyce travelled to Zurich in April 1930 for a consultation with Professor Alfred Vogt, a renowned Swiss oculist. The prognosis was better than expected and Joyce was asked to return in May to undergo an operation for tertiary cataract in his left eye. The surgery took place on 15 May 1930. While convalescing, he began desultorily to collect new notes which he entered into N38 (VI.B.32). Nora (his wife) and Helen Fleischman (his future daughter-in-law) read to him. One of the books involved was Vladimir Jabotinsky's *Samson the Nazarite* (this book was later to form the basis for a classic Hollywood epic starring Victor Mature).[1] Joyce would have been justified in seeing himself (as he probably did) as a latter-day Samson, laid low by his enemies and by the virtual loss of his sight. On the last point, however, he was on the road to recovery and, with Vogt's help, he would soon recover his sight sufficiently for him to be able to read and write. What he did not suspect was that a second affliction — in the person of his daughter Lucia — was waiting in the wings: her sad fate was destined to blight the remaining years of his life.

Although he continued to take notes, filling up first N38

---

[1] See Vincent Deane, "*Samson the Nazarite* in VI.B.32", *A Finnegans wake circular* 4 (1989), pp.51-55.

and starting on N39 (no longer extant), he did not feel up to tackling the "children's games" episode until the middle of October, well over four years after he had first made a plan of the piece. The original of this can be found on a page of manuscript (BL Add.MS 47482a-2) dating from May/June 1926:

△ night!
Driftwood on △. Trunkles. Contredanse. Hornies [cops] & Robbers. ⊤ devil ⌐. ⊥ angel ∧. ⊥ prisoner. The guess. (Pascal). Tug of love. ⊥ falls. ⌐ hide.
⊓ beholds. ◯ chuchotant. △ picks up. Croon Nasceià in melo. ⋈ ab. ☐ & ◯ round dance. Mulberry Bush. Colin Maillard. ⌐ blindfold. ☐. ✕ vident.
⊓ all in!

———

Interior of hotel. ◯
Paschal lambtable ⊓ fights △ (formerly)
Studies ⫝̸ [Shem, Shaun and Issy]
⊥ tells story in bed to ⌐

In the above, line 1 repeats the last word ("night!") of *Anna Livia* (I.8), lines 2 to 9 present a relatively detailed outline plan for the "children's games" (II.1) and lines 10-13 briefly describe Joyce's early ideas for II.2-3. As it is unlikely that Joyce had this plan to hand when he began the composition of II.1, it does not accurately reflect his actual construction of the piece, although many of the ideas included do feature. No longer writing for *transition*, Joyce intended the piece to be first published as an *édition de luxe* under the title *Chapelle d'Izzied* and he arranged for Adrienne Monnier's sister Marie, an accomplished designer of tapestries, to do a "hieroglyph" or "pictorial" preface. After he had written the first section, he described the "new" plan to Harriet Weaver in a letter dated 22 November 1930:

> The scheme of the piece ... is the game we used to call Angels and Devils or colours. The Angels, girls, are grouped behind the Angel, Shawn, and the Devil has to come over three times and ask for a colour. If the colour he asks for has been chosen by any girl she has to run and he tries to catch her. As far as I have written he has come twice and been twice baffled. The piece is full of rhythms taken from English singing games. When first baffled vindictively he thinks of publishing blackmail stuff about his father, mother etc etc etc. The second time he maunders off into sentimental poetry of what I actually wrote at the age of nine: "My cot alas that dear old shady home where oft in youthful sport I played, upon thy verdant grassy fields all day or lingered for a moment in thy bosom shade etc etc etc etc." This is interrupted by a violent pang of toothache after which he throws a fit. When he is baffled a second time the girl angels sing a hymn of liberation round Shawn. The page enclosed is still another version of a beautiful sentence from Edgar Quinet which I already refashioned in *transition* part one beginning "since the days of Hiber and Hairyman etc." E.Q. says that the wild flowers on the ruins of Carthage Numancia etc. have survived the political rises and downfall of Empires. In this case the wild flowers are the lilts of children.
>
> (*Letters I* 295)

At this point he paused. Working excruciatingly slowly (the words came out, he said, "like drops of blood"), he had managed to complete no more than sixteen handwritten pages. For the next few months he did no more than collect notes for the episode, filling up N39, N40 (VI.B.28B) and N41 (VI.B.33). In addition, he reorganized two or three of the older notebooks by transferring selected unused elements to SD1 (the "Scribbledehobble" notebook). Such an amount of reading, he complained to Harriet Weaver, "seems to be necessary before my old flying machine grumbles up into the air" (*Letters I* 300). On 4 March 1931 he sent her a sample list of the variety of books that were being read to him: "Marie Corelli, Swedenborg, St Thomas, the Sudanese war, Indian outcasts, Women under English Law, a description of St. Helena, Flammarion's The End of the World, scores of children's singing games from Germany, France, England and Italy and so on" (*Letters I* 302).[1] Despite all this reading and copying (Shem's favourite occupation), he was able to add less than half as much again to the draft of the "children's games" that he had sent to Miss Weaver, with the result that by April 1931, when he gave up his flat and moved his entire household to England, he had composed no more than twenty-odd pages of an episode planned four years earlier and for which he had spent nearly a year gathering notes.

There can be no doubt but that James Joyce was suffering from a severe case of what is commonly termed "writer's block". The syndrome, which evidently had its origins in the series of rejections beginning with the *Dial*'s in September 1926, was reinforced by the collapse of his sight in 1928, and was brought to a head by the increasing pressures from his

[1] For a detailed commentary on the use of three of these, see Danis Rose and John O'Hanlon, "Constructing *Finnegans wake*: three indexes", *A wake newlitter* XVII (1980), pp.3-15.

family which climaxed in 1930. The central issue was the status of his marriage. This was compelled by the engagement of his son Giorgio to Helen Fleischman: the "inheritance" had to be legally secured. Next, Lucia took up the gauntlet and in several violent outbursts berated her parents' marital irresponsibility. Joyce, in his weakened condition, caved in. He tried to make the best of it by pretending that he had already married Nora in 1904 (presumably in Trieste or Pola).[1] The fact remains, however, that the "second" marriage (which took place on 4 July 1931) was a deeply humiliating experience for James Joyce. In 1904, he had made it a point of honour *not* to enter into a formal marriage contract with Nora; a quarter of a century later, in post-operative stress and writing a book that nobody either wanted or understood (least of all his family), he could no longer "flash his antlers in the air" but rather, with head bent, had to "adequate the balance-sheet".

His personal moral courage was tested a second time some six months later, and was again found wanting. On 22 December 1931 his father, John Stanislaus Joyce, took seriously ill and was taken to hospital. For the previous twelve years the old man had lived as a paying guest with a Protestant family, the Medcalfs, at 25 Claude road, Glasnevin. Albert Medcalf wrote at once to Joyce and explained the situation. He added: "I would suggest to you to write to your father by return as I don't think he will last very long, and as you know his heart is centred on you, and his last words before I left him last night

[1]   See *Letters III* 222. While no evidence for this marriage has ever been produced, the Joyces did celebrate the anniverary of their "nuptials" on 8 October each year. On that date in 1904 they were on a steamship on the Irish Sea and nowhere near either Pola or Trieste.

were, Don't forget to write to Jim". The unspoken message from father to son was clear:

I am dying. Come home. Father.

To his shame, he did not go. "I did not feel myself safe and my wife and son opposed my going", he explained to T.S. Eliot (*Letters I* 311). John Joyce died on 29 December 1931 and was buried two days later. At the funeral, his illustrious son was represented by a wreath and a card, inscribed "With Sorrow and Love." Two weeks later Joyce wrote to Harriet Weaver: "The weeks since have been passed in prostration of mind ... I am thinking of abandoning work altogether and leaving the thing unfinished with blanks. Worries and jealousies and my own mistakes. Why go on writing about a place I did not dare to go to at such a moment ...?".

In the event "the thing" did manage, against these insuperable odds — the penman's physical and moral collapse — to get finished. Even so, apart from a brief period at the very end (like Samson's), James Joyce was never again to experience the creative bursts, the rapid succession of ideas, the free flow of episode after episode that characterized his work on *Finn's hotel* and on parts I and III of *Finnegans wake*. It is in this context that we should judge his pathetic attempts to have someone else finish the book for him (we know of two people that he approached: Thomas MacGreevy and James Stephens) and his almost manic promotion (during this same period) of the tenor John Sullivan. It is in this context also that we should understand his implacable resolve against all advice (including his wife and son's) never to admit defeat in the case of his daughter Lucia's descent into madness. It is as if he said to himself, Never again.

To return to our narrative; other than collecting more notes, which he entered into N42 (VI.B.31), Joyce did little work during his five months in England. On his return to Paris in the autumn of 1931 he evaded working on II.1 by undertaking the revision (for eventual book publication) of part I. This revision, which coincided with the compilation of the first half of N43 (VI.B.35), was completed in the spring. He then stopped working. In July 1932 (a year after signing the contract) he offered to return to Faber and Faber the advance given him.

In August, Eugene Jolas encouraged him to finish the "children's games" by offering to publish it in *transition*. Joyce's mood lightened and he resumed work, but in a very laboured manner. As is evidenced by the extant documents — and, indeed, by the very absence of many pages — he worked by composing small fragments and threading them together end to end. These juxtapositions he then revised in an extraordinarily complex and convolute manner.[1] Although he used many of his older notebooks in this revision, Joyce also compiled the second half of N43 (VI.B.35) during this period.

One of the notable features of the episode (which was published in *transition* in February 1933) was added late in the composition: this is the pantomime "programme" which opens the piece and which supplied the new title *The mime of Mick, Nick and the Maggies* under which it was published as an *édition de luxe* in 1934 (but without the Marie Monnier preface; Adrienne Monnier and Sylvia Beach had in the meantime severed relations with Joyce). By transforming the piece into a children's play, he was of course mindful of III.4, the adults' play, the front door of part II thereby matching the backdoor of part III.

[1] See pages 111-198 of the *James Joyce archive* volume for *Finnegans wake* Book II, Chapter One.

10 Night studies (II.2): how a chapter ate itself

When, at the beginning of 1933, he had finished with the "children's games" (II.1), Joyce turned to the "studies" episode, the central section of which ("the triangle") he had composed in 1926 and revised in 1928 for *transition*. His task seemed on the surface a relatively simple one: compose an introduction to and an ending for the piece and make sure that Issy (who hardly features in "the triangle") has a speaking part. In much the same bitty way as he had finished II.1, he began by drafting separate small fragments of text which he hoped would subsequently fit together. This time, however, things were destined to go seriously awry; two and a half years were to pass before the "opening and closing" sections were to be published in *transition*, and another two and a half before the composition of the episode was complete.

During 1932, and following the breach with Sylvia Beach, Paul Léon emerged as the most important person in James Joyce's life, at least in so far as his wellbeing and work were concerned. Confidant, legal adviser, agent, manager, secretary, friend, surrogate—none of these words on its own adequately defines his function. As Joyce stumbled through the 1930s, Léon propped him up. Playing Shem to Joyce's ALP, he even took to writing to Harriet Weaver listing the author's woes. In this, as the recently opened files in the National Library of Ireland attest, he invariably followed Joyce's detailed instructions, adding only tact and restraint.

For example, on 4 April 1933 he wrote: "You know as well as I do the character of his work the difficulties of it the repeated lapses into loss of confidence which they provoke in him. Considering all this I am afraid that he does not get not only sufficient but even enough encouragement from his immediate surroundings". Three weeks later he quotes Joyce as declaring, "Let everything go to pieces!" Alas, that is precisely what happened to the fragments of the "studies" that he was composing at the time.

The first piece of text which Joyce drafted is coded II.2 section 4 in the *James Joyce archive*; he originally intended to open the chapter with it. The preceding chapter, II.1, ends with the abrupt termination of the children's play on the streets of the village with their being called home to do their homework. The first draft of this new piece was compiled by an amalgamation of textual elements from SD1 (the "Scribbledehobble" notebook). In its protoform, it begins in mid-studies:

> Scribbledehobbles are at their pensums. Trifid tongue and dove without gall to solve dulcarnon's dire dilemma what stumped bold Alexander and drove him to pulfer turnips. But what a world of weariness is theirs! For how many guildens would one walk now to the pillar? For one hundred? For one hundred's thousand? And to what will't all serve them in an after world.

Though quite short, the section was faircopied, typed, revised and retyped twice. In its final form it began "While way back home in Pacata Hibernia" followed by a description of the interior of the hotel and a short scene involving HCE and ALP (as in the 1926 plan: see page 111).

Working backwards toward the present start, Joyce next added a lyrical description of Chapelizod and environs (section 2, now *FW* 264-266.19), made up almost entirely out of the "Chapelizod" entry in Thom's *Dublin directory*, and beginning, "In these places sojournamous". He next drafted the present opening, in which the tavern is approached (as it happens, by bicycle) street by street. Joyce then drafted a piece (the present section 3) dealing with Issy which apparently was to follow the "Scribbledehobble" fragment (the first written). Though the precise order of their composition is unknown, it was also around this time (the summer of 1933) that he wrote the very short sections 6 (Issy's letter), 7 (yet another version — this time a *verbatim* transcription — of Edgar Quinet's piece about the ruins and the flowers) and 9 (the close).

Joyce paused at this point leaving the episode unfinished and unintegrated, much as he had done with II.1. A year passed in which, other than a first round of revisions on part III, he did hardly any work at all. Even his notetaking slowed down: in the years 1933 and 1934 he compiled only three notebooks, N44 (VI.B.34), N45 (VI.B.43) and N46 (VI.B.36).

In July 1934 Joyce quit his flat on the rue de la Galilée (which he had never particularly liked) and left for a holiday in Belgium and an extended stay in Switzerland. He started to work again on the "studies" in the autumn while he was in Zurich. Once again, the prompt was the opportunity to publish the episode (or rather its opening and closing parts) in *transition*. In putting the various sections together, for some unaccountable reason (he no longer liked them or, perhaps, he had forgotten to bring all the manuscript with him) he omitted sections 4 (the "Scribbledehobble piece"), 6 and 7 (Issy's letter and the Quinet fragment). This extraordinary indecisiveness and/or forgetfulness is characteristic of Joyce in the 1930s and accounts in a large measure for the apparent impenetrableness of the texts he composed during these years.

It was in Zurich also that he came up with the idea of the present odd format of the episode, with its marginalia and footnotes. This was done ostensibly to give the chapter the appearance of a schoolchild's scrawled on textbook; to me it makes it look more like one of his revised typescripts. As a final touch, he added the children's "nightletter"[1] which was intended to appear on a page of its own after the "night studies" and thereby at the dead centre of the book.

It took Joyce several further months to complete the fragment (still minus some of its parts), which is quite short, and it appeared in *transition* in July 1935. The story does not end there, however. More than two years later, in November/ December 1937, in a sort of dress rehearsal for what was to happen to *Finn's hotel*, Joyce took out or found the abandoned or forgotten sections 4, 6 and 7. He did not know what to do with them. Hating waste, he broke up the "Scribbledehobble" piece into its constituent elements and constructed an entirely new fragment (Section 5: *FW* 275.03-279.09), to which he added section 6 as a footnote and appended Section 7. All in all, it was not the optimal, nor the original, arrangement of the parts.

---

[1]   This rather sinister missive with its "youlldied greedings" from the children takes its title from "night telegraph letters", a cheaper form of telegram that Joyce used at the time in communicating from Switzerland.

11   *Scene in the public* (II.3§1-5)

In the spacious, more congenial atmosphere of 7 rue Edmond Valentin, into which he moved in February 1935, Joyce's circumstances slowly began to improve. As the flat was unfurnished, he was able to take his belongings (including the bulk of his books) out of storage. The periods of remission from the black moods in which he was unable to write increased both in duration and in strength. Nevertheless, a full year was to pass before he was able to sit down to compose the third episode of part II, which nine years earlier he had described to Harriet Weaver as "a scene in the public", meaning, of course, in the public bar.

With II.2 out of the way (at least for the time being), Joyce returned to part III and, over several sessions during 1935 and early 1936, completed his revision. For this work, he made extensive use of the transcriptions of old notebooks which Madame France Raphael was preparing for him on a regular basis. He also filled in, though slowly, N47 (VI.B.40), compiled between February 1935 and early 1936. It is only in the last pages of this notebook that we find the first intimations of II.3 (specifically, the first section of the episode), namely a few units tagged "Kersse", the name of a Dublin tailor; e.g., "Jerkin (Kersse)" and "gusset sewer (Kersse)" (166, 179). These notes continue in the early pages of N48 (VI.B.38); e.g., the significant "Kersse's d. [daughter] liked foreigners" (22). It is probable that Joyce composed an early draft of II.3§1 at this time (early 1936); the earliest draft of the piece that has survived is a fair copy dating from the summer of 1936 which was manifestly copied from an earlier version.

At this point it is worthwhile giving an overview of the first five sections of II.3, all of which take place in the bar of Earwicker's hotel. These are:

> **Section 1**: a radio broadcast of the tale of Pukklesen (a hunchbacked Norwegian Captain), Kersse (a tailor) and McCann (a ship's husband) in which, *inter alia*, the story is told of how HCE met and married ALP.

> **Sections 2-3**: an interruption in which Kate (the cleaning woman) tells HCE that he is wanted upstairs, the door is closed and the tale of Buckley is introduced.

> **Sections 4-5**: the tale, recounted by Butt and Taff (Shem and Shaun) and beamed over the televison, of how Buckley shot the Russian General (HCE).

Joyce turned to I.1 ("the prelude") for the basic format of the episode, which thus contains strong echoes of the Wellington museum piece, the Prankquean sequence and the Mutt and Jute "after the battle" dialogue. Significantly, just as he was getting started on II.3, he returned to part I, made some last-minute revisions to the copy for Faber and Faber, and entered notes *from* its text into N48.

Joyce described section 1 of the new chapter to Louis Gillet in a letter dated 5 June 1936:

> I have worked all this time on a chapter which is perhaps the most complacently absurd thing that I ever did until now. I

gave it up during these last weeks. I was too depressed to
continue the buffoonery. But starting tomorrow I shall set
to work again. It is the story of a captain ... and a Dublin
tailor which my god-father told me forty years ago, trying to
explain the arrival of my Viking in Dublin, his marriage, and
a lot of things I don't care to mention here.[1]

Working relatively smoothly for a change, Joyce finished
the marriage section by December 1936. His notetaking also
increased in volume; he had completed N49 and compiled
most of N50 (VI.B.37) before he finished. He added a new
opening sentence — "It maynot or maybe a no concern of
the Guinnesses but" — based on the title, *No concern of the
Guinnesses?*, which he gave to the publication of I.2§1
(the original Earwicker fragment) in a selection from his
work in progress which he published in a book entitled
transition stories (edited by Robert Sage and Eugene
Jolas) in 1929.[2]

As soon as he had despatched section 1 to *transition* in
December 1936 (it appeared, after some delay, in May
1937), and although he still had the proofs of the fragment to
correct, Joyce immediately set to work on the shorter
transitional section 2 and on a first draft of section 4, the Butt
and Taff dialogue. He stopped early in 1937, however, and
concentrated on the galley proofs of parts I and III which
began to arrive in the spring. He worked assiduously on these
during the remainder of the year, during which he also

[1] From Georges Markow-Totevy's translation of Louis Gillet, *Claybook
for James Joyce* (London and New York: Abelard-Schuman, 1958).
[2] The opening sentence of this fragment is "Now, concerning the
genesis of Harold or Humphrey Chimpden's occupational agnomen".
(The recycling was effected via a note on p.120 of N50.)

compiled notebooks N51 (VI.B.44) and N52 (VI.B.42). He only got back to work on "Butt and Taff" in the winter, finishing it on 20 January 1938. His initial plan was to bypass publication in *transition* and send the piece directly to Faber and Faber, but at the last minute he changed his mind and decided to collaborate in what turned out to be the last issue of Jolas's review.

This dialogue, which nicely balances the tale of the Norwegian Captain, focusses on the assassination of the Russian General (HCE again) by Buckley (a version of the Cad) and is intimately connected with the incident in the park as recounted in part I of the book. In early 1938 he added a coda (section 5), based on the Russian and Irish revolutions and composed almost entirely from elements in the "Bolshevism" and "1916" indexes in N53 (VI.B.46). In this, the sole example in the text of Shem and Shaun fusing into a single entity, Butt and Taff become "two and the same man".

12 Lights out in the village
(II.3§6-7 and II.4)

From 1926/1927, Joyce evidently intended four episodes in part II of his book, as there were four in part III, thereby collectively balancing the eight episodes of part I (the single episode of part IV was to be by way of *ricorso*). This affords a neat fourfold symmetry 4/4 — 4 — 4 (— 1). What, then, was Joyce's original idea for II.4, the fourth episode of part II? As published, II.4 is a composite of two stories from the *Finn's hotel* suite. But if, as I have argued elsewhere, Joyce decided only at the last minute to interpolate into *Finnegans wake* the *Finn's hotel* pieces (suitably wracked to fit), does this not leave a vacuum in Joyce's own conceptualization, namely, the original plan for II.4?

The answer is that it does not. The fourth and final episode of part II as originally envisaged was not only planned and carefully considered (notes were taken for it), it was actually written. In the notebooks it went by the title of "○". It was planned to centre on the reaction of the Twelve (the customers/jurors) to the stories about HCE recounted in the barroom scene (i.e., the Norwegian Captain and the Russian General tales) and on HCE's own self-vindication. Just as these stories are closely connected with the early history of Earwicker and the crime in the park as rehearsed in part I, the "debate" involving the Twelve harks back to the gossip and to the trials that followed.

The twelve customers, as earlier demonstrated, were very

late in coming into the picture and arrived pre-coded as $\bigcirc$,
most originally in the notes on the last page of N18 (dated July-
September 1925) and in the text as part of the opening scene in
III.4. In the latter, in prototextual form, they are described so:

> every night while twelve good men & true in their numbered
> habitations tried him [HCE] over in their minds & found
> him guilty on the imputation of fornication minus copulation
> or if 'twere not so, deretane denudation with intent to
> excitation of firearmed forces of the nation but with family
> pressures as mitigation and in any case he being worthy of
> remuneration for his having displayed so much toleration,
> reprobate and all as he was, in respects to his high station
> more especially as he was suffering from a medical
> attestation having only strength enough to implore for all
> concerned the curses of coagulation for, by all that's holy,
> if he was offensive to the nostrils on the other side has
> distinctly the eye's delectation but, summing him up
> exaltation is no contravention to our statute & common
> legislation so three months for the pest of the park, as
> per act one, section two, schedule three of the first of
> King Jark, this sentence to be carried out tomorrow
> morn at six o'clock shark & may the hail of mercy on his
> hurlyburlygrowth. Amen says the Clerk!

As new protagonists in their own right, the twelve good men
appear hereafter in the notebooks in variously predicated
form; for example, "the boys $\bigcirc$" (N21), "$\bigcirc$ zodiac" (N22),
"$\bigcirc$ 12 Galway tribes" (N25) and "$\bigcirc$ pomes penyeach"
(N42). In the text, they also appear in the portrait gallery of
the questionnaire (I.6) written in the summer of 1927, where
they occupy the seventh frame as the "components parts of

our whole" who "unify their voxes in our voice of vaticin-
ation". It was only later that Joyce decided to memorialize
them with an episode to themselves. The first inkling of this
appears in N42 (VI.B.31), dating from April-November
1931, on p.269 of which Joyce breaks down the "hours" of
part II:

8-9	Children's hour	[II.1: the "children's games]
9-10	A little learning	[II.2: "night studies"]
10-11	hist. survey	[II.3§1-5 : the stories about HCE]
11-12	open air debate	[the original II.4: the Twelve discuss HCE]

Certainly, this is a tentative scheme; but there is immediately
afterwards a shift in the use of ○ in the notebooks away from
simple predication to theme or episode notions. In N43
(VI.B.35), compiled in 1932, one finds *inter alia* "○ discuss
impotence" (24), "○ lights go out" (51), and "drunken ○"
(131) — themes which are expounded in the drafts of the
original II.4. Moreover, in Joyce's letter of 7 June 1926
(quoted earlier) the notion of a "lights out" in the village is
specifically stated by Joyce to constitute the last of the
episodes for part II:

> Between the close of △ at nightfall and ∧a there are three or
> four other episodes, the children's games, night studies, a
> scene in the "public", and a "lights out in the village".

It should be noted that this plan is rather compact, spanning
exactly the period in which the lights, lit at the start of the
children's games, illuminate the little village of Chapelizod.

Notes for the as-yet-unwritten fourth episode continue to appear in subsequent notebooks: for example, in N44 (VI.B.34, compiled in the first half of 1933) we find "◯ talks about mesmerism" (36), "◯ writing letters all night" (84), "◯ discuss the Pleistocene ice of ∧c" (158) and "◯ adopt ⊓ as ancestor" (107). A similar pattern is found in later notebooks.

Joyce began to write the fourth episode of part II at the end of 1937, just as he was completing the "Butt and Taff" piece. He was working at full belt, and still hoped to have the book finished by his fifty-sixth birthday on 2 February 1938.[1] Writing to Faber and Faber on 18 December 1937, Paul Léon explained in detail the make-up of part II. It was to consist of four episodes. The first and second (II.1 and II.2) had already been sent to London. Episode 3 was to consist of two sections (i.e., the Norwegian Captain and the Russian General), the first of which (in the form of a revised copy of the *transition* 26 pages) Léon was including with his letter, and the second of which (in typescript form: at this stage Joyce had not yet decided to send it to Jolas for *transition* 27) he would send in a week or two. The fourth episode was to follow in due course. On 4 January 1938 he wrote again, stating that Faber and Faber now had three fourths of part II[2] and that Joyce was working away at top speed on the fourth and final episode.

What is now II.3§6-7 (apart from the first few lines beginning "Shutmup", which announced closing-time and

---

[1] Had this come about, it is probable that the *Finnegans wake* which would have come into the world would have done so without the *Finn's hotel* appendages adhering to it.

[2] In point of fact, Faber and Faber had received no more than two-thirds of part II. The discrepancy arose because neither Joyce nor Léon at that time had yet envisaged the addition of the *Finn's hotel* pieces.

which Joyce at first intended to close II.3),[1] the present *third* part of the penultimate episode of part II, was originally written to constitute by itself the fourth and final episode. The text on which Joyce was working at the beginning of 1938 and to which Léon refers was the present II.3§6. In this section, Earwicker returns from upstairs, "regrouped", remassed and reconstituted (described in terms of a condensation from Magellanic clouds and a subsequent expansion, as of the universe) after the fragmentation brought about by his "assassination" (described as an atomic explosion) by Buckley. He addresses himself to his fellow men and assents "This is true", admits that he chose his own name (that of an insect) and poses a riddle (a version of Shem's "riddle of the universe" from I.7: *When is a man not a man?*). He then recounts an experience he had while reading a book (apparently *Ulysses*) as he relieved himself in an outside jakes and declares his conviction, corroborated by the latest written reports, that he is considered "big altogether". A piece on heresy (Pelagius) and a musical interlude, the "dewfolded song of the naughtingels" (a twofold form of the naughty Issy), follow. Immediately thereafter, the Twelve come into prominence: "The all of them the pig village boys in that smoker, a sixdigitarian legion, the Clandibblon cartel, foursquare in condomnation ... rally agreed". In response, HCE unashamedly admits his guilt but nonetheless tries, without success, to excuse himself.

Completely exhausted, and with the prospect of having his book published on 4 July 1938 (his father's birthday) finally impossibilized, Joyce stopped work. He travelled to Switzerland in early February to see Vogt and to rest. While

---

[1] An inspection of the original manuscripts confirms this: see vol 55 of the *James Joyce archive*.

in Zurich, he started to work on IV (the final, shorter part of the book). Then, in June, he averted again to part II and began to put into order for the printer the second half of II.3 (i.e., §2-5) and what he *still* regarded as II.4 (i.e., II.3§6). On 24 June, he sent II.3§2-5 to Faber and Faber. From Faber's reply (27 June) we know that these passages were described as "additional matter at the *end* [italics mine] of episode 3". In July he remembered the "Roderick O'Conor" piece, which he had for some time kept in abeyance but in mind (see earlier chapters) as a close for episode 4 of part II. He went to fetch it. Delving into his files, he found *Finn's hotel*.[1] That is to say, he found more than he bargained for.

Alongside the "O'Conor" piece, he found the "St Kevin" sketch, the "Letter", and the "Mamalujo" piece (which he had termed "a sidepiece" in 1924 at the time of its publication in the *Transatlantic review*). While he could use the "St Kevin" and the "Letter" in part IV, "Mamalujo" caused a serious problem. What could he do with it? As said before, he hated to waste anything. Yet, with almost all of the book already typeset, his options were limited. His solution was to revise it, have it typed, and position it at the end of part II. As it did not at all fit in with the "II.4" that he had already written, he had no choice but to append *that* to the end of II.3, making that episode inordinately long and complex.

In late July 1938, and now with IV in mind — he was working on the two (or rather three) episodes at the same time — he remembered St Kevin's counterpart, the "St Patrick" sketch, his copy of which had been lost. Léon wrote

---

[1]   From an unpublished letter to Harriet Weaver of 10 September 1923, we know that Joyce kept the *Finn's hotel* pieces (or what he retained of them) in a special folder. Miss Weaver kept her copy (which was more complete) in a large brown envelope.

to Harriet Weaver to ask if she had a copy. She had. To Joyce's consternation, she added that there was a fourth piece that she had herself typed out in 1923 when Joyce was in Bognor, promising to send it on if Léon would tell her which pieces Joyce already had. It took three weeks to sort the problem out. The extra piece turned out to be the "Tristan and Isolde" story from *Finn's hotel*, about which Joyce had completely forgotten. The best he could do with it was to tear it apart and add the fragments to "Mamalujo". The "new II.4" which emerged is a rather forced composite of the two pieces which in their original forms are radically different in mood, style and technique.

To facilitate the inclusion of "Roderick O'Conor" in the "old II.4" (now part of II.3), Joyce composed II.3§7 in which Sigurdsen — cast as a policeman — arrives to send the drunken customers home and to ensure that Earwicker is locked inside. The Twelve leave, reluctantly, but before they disperse they accuse, berate and condemn Earwicker from outside the pub. Inside HCE (now portrayed as an aged King Roderick) cleans up and drinks what remains in the glasses left behind them by the customers. (This last is somewhat inconsistent with the still-strong thirst expressed by the departing guests, who demand more alcohol.) In any event, the section, and thereby the original part II, ends with Earwicker passing out under the influence of drink.

The thus newly constituted closing episodes of part II were not ready to be sent to Faber and Faber until 14 November 1938. By then, part IV was also ready.

13 Kevin's orisons: the end (IV)

In 1938, twelve years after he had first outlined the plan of the piece, Joyce began to work on "K's orisons". On 16 February of that year, while still on holiday in Zurich, he informed Paul Léon that he had started to work slowly on the aubade, or dawnsong, which was to end his book. As planned, it follows directly after III.4 ("Shaun-d") and, in the faircopy (the earliest extant manuscript), opens appropriately:

> Calling all dawns. Calling all dawns to dayne.

Progress was slow at first, but soon gathered momentum. In addition to composing IV, Joyce was also working on the conclusion to part II and revising and returning the galley proofs of the other parts of the book. For this latter work, he used principally N53 (VI.B.46) and N54 (VI.B.45) and several of the transcriptions made by Madame Raphael; but for IV, or rather the first section thereof, the important notebook, N55, compiled between March and August 1938, is missing. We can, nevertheless, determine at least part of its content: it contained *inter alia* notes on Sanskrit, Samoyed, New Ireland and the Bismarck Archipelago, extracts from a genealogical article in the *Weekly Irish Times* on the Finnegan family, and material from Oliver St John Gogarty's *I follow St Patrick*.

As explained in the previous chapter, Joyce dismantled the *Finn's hotel* suite in July 1938. The "St Kevin" sketch, while having nothing to do with dawn — treating as it does with baptism and meditation — slotted in nicely enough after Kevin's (i.e. Shaun's, *not* St Kevin's) orisons. "St Patrick", a copy of which he received from Harriet Weaver in late July, went conveniently in next and was "introduced" by a third Mutt and Jeff dialogue, loosely based on information from Gogarty's book. He was still working on these two sections in August when, once again on holiday in Switzerland, he started to compile N56 (VI.B.41).

Joyce justified to others the inclusion of the two saintly vignettes in IV by conjuring up the idea of the first rays of morning sunshine lighting up a stained-glass triptych in Chapelizod parish church. Comes the question, What about the third image? In the book, the third panel of the triptych — depicting St Laurence O'Toole, the archbishop of Dublin, welcoming Henry II in a.d. 1171 on his arrival to secure the city for England — takes up scarcely a line of text. When he heard about the existence of another, unnamed piece from the *Finn's hotel* suite, did he perhaps think or hope it might be another saint. Alas, neither Tristan nor Isolde (who turned up in late August) were particularly saintly or suitable for IV.

With sections 1-3 written (the dawnsong, the Kevin and the Patrick passages), the original plan for part IV was effectively completed. But he still had Dame Anna Livia Plurabelle Earwicker's letter. What was he to do with it? What he did was to take it apart, rework and revise it and put it in after the Patrick section, where it now sits, uncomfortable and incongruous. It has frankly nothing to do with dawn or endings.

This left only one thing unseen to: journey's end. The very last thing. Written in a short, last burst of creative energy in the winter of 1938, Anna Livia's final monologue, her farewell and his, transcends anything that Joyce had ever written before. Anna Livia, grown old and weary, relinquishes everything that connects her to the living, even her name. All is lost; but a last leaf clings still, a breath, to remind her of. As she thinks back fondly on her girlhood the unheeding tides sweep her into the wind-tossed sea where the wild ones, the barking sea-hags of the waves, wait to claim her; and she runs to her cold sea-father, a small sea-girt girl-child once again, his only, into his arms.

N57 (VI.B.47) was compiled specially for this section. Much more than any of the other notebooks, it contains original compositions of many of the passages in the "Soft morning" finale. One particular passage in the notebook (p.40) tells us, if we need to be told, that whilst ostensibly the piece describes a young girl rushing into the arms of her father, it was also James Joyce, after so many years, reaching out for his mother:

> *and old it's sad*
> *and old it's sad*
> *and weary mother*
> *I go back to you*

Near the beginning of another book, there is a telling scene:

> Stephen stood up and went over to the parapet. Leaning on it he looked down on the water and on the mailboat clearing the harbourmouth of Kingstown.
> — Our mighty mother! Buck Mulligan said.
> He turned abruptly his grey searching eyes from the sea to Stephen's face.
> — The aunt thinks you killed your mother, he said.

When he had finished the monologue and, with it, his book,
Joyce went down to the banks of the river Seine and, looking
down on the water, wept bitter tears. Nearly sixteeen years
had passed since he had first put pen to paper and written the
"Roderick O'Conor" piece of *Finn's hotel*. He had been then
at the height of his powers and fame: he was the author of
Ulysses. Harriet Weaver's munificence was not yet eaten
away. His friends, his peers and his family had not yet lost
faith in his work. His health was not yet shattered. Yet he had
done it. Ha ha ha! This strange laughter he put into a yet
stranger letter which he forged for Léon to send to Miss
Weaver as if from him. His book, it relates, has nothing to say
about the serious and pressing issues of the day. It is a work
of the most colossal triviality. He has acted according to his
conscience. It is done.

Nothing remained but to tidy up. N58 (VI.B.30) was used
in the final corrections to the last of the galleys. A specially
bound copy of the book was delivered to him on his fifty-
seventh birthday, 2 February 1939. On 4 May, the two hundred and fortieth anniversary of the setting sail from Bristol of
the *Antelope* (destination the South Sea), *Finnegans wake*
was launched in London and New York, to no great fanfare.

But he was not yet entirely free of the book. He made a
few notes for the "correction" of the text and entered them
into N59 (VI.B.48), the first of the post-*Wake* notebooks. To
help him with this task of correction, Faber and Faber sent
him on 30 August an *unbound* copy of *Finnegans wake*.[1] As
this made its way to Paris, the Germans invaded Poland and
Joyce was once again swamped in personal problems. Lucia
had to be moved to safety. Then the marriage of Giorgio and

[1]   This, and not — as posited by Spielberg — the book sent for his birthday, is the copy (catalogued VI.H.4.a) at Buffalo.

Helen collapsed. Nora, who was very close to her son, took Giorgio's side and persuaded Joyce likewise. Paul Léon did not agree, and a rift developed between the two men. In the summer of 1940, at Saint Gérand-le-Puy, they were reconciled, and worked together to complete the "correction" of the text (but actually achieving little more than a touching up of the punctuation). In September, Léon and Joyce said goodbye, one doomed man to another.

The last of the extant notebooks, N60 (VIII.C.2), is little more than a pocket diary for 1940. Nevertheless, the leopard being unable to change his spots, it contains the usual words and phrases, from "jeepers creepers" to "mouche". Last of all, on the back cover, in sinister parody of his innocent little signs, mindful perhaps of serious and pressing issues, there are three attempts, rather childish, to inscribe a swastika.

III

Technical

14 Editing indexes: conventions

As we have earlier affirmed, the notebooks consist of a very long string of discrete, usually disconnected indexes. Interspersed with these, but exceptionally, are occasional bits and pieces of a different nature. Throughout the indexes, also, we find the signatures of a family of curious little signs that Joyce invented to designate his protagonists: these hieroglyphs have been discussed in detail in earlier chapters. But if we wish to delve beneath the surface of *Finnegans wake* — if we wish to understand it in its complementarity, as it were *in both planes of reference*, contextually (intratextually) and intertextually, and if we wish to know what Joyce was contemplating in the post-*Ulysses* years — it is of prime importance to identify the multiple sources of the indexes, relate the units in the indexes to these and also to the text of *Finnegans wake* in progress.[1] A not insignificant amount of research towards this end has already been done,

[1] In this context I should like to quote the sentiments of Fredson Bowers, late dean of textual scholarship: "Though a poem, like a man, may stand rejoicing in finished maturity, we must surely understand it with superior intimacy if we have watched its growth and seen its perfection in the very act of shaping. There is such a thing as love, I should urge, in our response to a perfect poem. The current games of intellectual chess, of subjectively drawn tensions, ambiguities, and *discordia concors*, too often overlook or overlay that simple act of love, which the textual critic may help us toward in his concern for the childhood and adolescence, awkward or charming, of the living seed of a writer" (*Textual and literary criticism*, 1959).

mainly by the Dublin/Antwerp school of textual scholars, but the greater body of indexes remains yet to be detected. To facilitate the unification in one centre of the research of different scholars carried out in different locations, some common conventions are desirable; some of these are described below along with a sample index. The different problems posed by the transcriptions are addressed in Chapter 16.

The simplest way, but an inadequate way, of editing a notebook is to produce a more or less diplomatic or literal transcription with little or no editorial apparatus. Thus, taking the first page of N1 (VI.B.10) — the first page of the archive we are concerned with here — this approach would produce something like the following.

N1 (VI.B.10):1
   Buttle I franking machine I son turned out badly I look at it over there I Ir cricket I Lambert Gwynn I horses I Widger I Beasley.

"Widger" and "son turned out badly" in the above are crossed through on the notebook page in red crayon. Familiarity with Joyce's practice leads one to realize that once he transferred a unit, such as "Widger" above, into a draft in progress (and into a new context) he crossed it through in coloured crayon. This was usually but not invariably the case, as one sporadically finds *transferred* elements uncrossed (by oversight) in the notebooks. Clearly Joyce, who returned to the notebooks for raw textual material on numerous occasions (and pointedly not by way of a single sweep through the units), wished to preclude his own duplication of usage. "Widger" was to go in once, and not twice. (Even here, Joyce was not quite consistent in that he compiled different indexes using the same sourcebook on more than one occasion — for example, *The house by the churchyard*, *The book of the dead*, and *The trees of Ireland* — thereby increasing the possibility of duplication. But these exceptions need not detain us here.) The edited page can be improved by including by way of superscript a colour-code and by citing (a) the unit's location in the final text, (b) the BL MS draft reference to the manuscript page (where extant) on which the transferred unit appears as auxesis or overlay (or in the base text), (c) the *James Joyce archive* volume and page reference to the same, and (d) the draft stage of the transference. This last reference should follow the coding devised by the *Archive* editors, namely: book.chapter§section.level (where, for example, II.1§1.*0 means *Finnegans wake* Book II, Chapter 1, Section 1, (autograph) level 0. The asterisk indicates that the draft is in its entirety written in the author's own hand. "Widger", accordingly, can now less nakedly be detailed as

   ʳWidger,
      FW 39.11 47472-140 *JJA45*:057
      I.2§2.3/3.3

This is a marked improvement, but the sense of the different words on the page remains ambiguous. What could they mean? What or who is "Buttle"? What is the inter-relationship, if any, between the various words? Is Buttle to be connected to Widger? Whose son turned out badly? Is it pointless to opine?

   In an unpublished paper, Geert Lernout has provided a splendid parodic, so-called expansive interpretation of this very page, indulging in unrestrained association to force the words into a pattern that relates to notions that might purportedly hold some significance for James Joyce. Of course, as Lernout makes clear, such an undertaking even if interesting or comic is absurd: as textual scholars we ought not be derailed by the octopus eisegesis (the description of one's response to a text). All that we can intelligently say about the above string of words is that, in accordance with the paradigm discussed earlier, they derive from some printed source the identification of which will adequately explain their meaning. The question of what Joyce did intellectually with the units *after he had gathered them* is a different matter entirely, and one that cannot properly be considered until *after* their source has been identified. As it so happens, that veteran sleuth Vincent Deane has traced these early units to late 1922 issues of *The Irish Times*: Joyce was jotting down what caught his eye as he skipped through the newspaper! Buttle, for example, that Janus of the notebooks, turns out to be Lieutenant Albert Edward Buttle, Royal Irish Rifles, who died in France on 2 October 1918 of wounds received in action.

Information as to the source context should always be included in a notebook edition, which thereby ceases to be an arcane and clinical interconcatenation of lifeless fragments, but lifts itself into a work of outstanding explanatory force. Consider, for example, *FW* 492.11f: "Mother of emeralds, ara poog neighbours!" What does this mean? (And we must remember that *Finnegans wake* contains thousands of sentences like this, with different levels of potential meaning, of all of which we must ask, What does this mean?) Clearly, the base meaning at the narrative level — the *use* that Joyce made of the elements that make up the sentence — is something like "Mother of God, *ora pro nobis*!", either a prayer or an expletive. That is the kind of meaning a good reader would pick up on a first reading when ideally he or she should not bother to stop at every potential lexical crux.[1] For a second reading, or preparation therefor (and *Finnegans wake* richly rewards rereading), something more is necessary. The second part, "ara poog neighbours!", probably does not require a notebook reference, as the title of Dion Boucicault's play *Arrah-na-pogue* comes to mind. "Mother of emeralds", however, is unlikely to be accurately glossed without tracing it back to its notebook source, N47 (VI.B.40):157, and identifying the index of which it forms a part. It is an invocation of Egyptian *Book of the dead* imagery and refers to an Uatch amulet made of mother-of-emerald (green feldspar) which was placed by the local priest at the neck of the deceased to secure for its (literally) nameless soul the protection of Isis and the fortitude of Horus in its perilous journey through the underworld.[2] In illustration of this fact-specific "theoretical dead end" type of index-editing, one could cite any one of dozens of papers, such as those

[1] There is, alas — and other than the annotational trap — a further serious handicap preventing a straightforward first reading of *Finnegans wake*: namely, the corrupt state of the text: the botched punctuation, the truncated sentences and the misplaced words, phrases and paragraphs. These problems, however, will be for the most part resolved on the publication of the reading text of the forthcoming critical edition.

[2] See Danis Rose, *Chapters of coming forth by day* (Colchester: A wake newlitter press, 1982), for an account of the total of nine *Book of the dead* indexes used in the composition of *Finnegans wake*. The precise extent of Joyce's use of Egyptian funerary texts — one of the most important sources that he had recourse to — is mapped out in the twenty-four pages of this short book. The sole alternative non-notebook oriented approach to identifying allusions is, at best, dubious reference-hunting in the quagmire of the final text, fumbling in the (book of the) dark, so to say.

which have appeared in *A wake newlitter* or the *Finnegans wake circular*. One such that is immediately to hand is Vincent Deane's edited version of Joyce's (admittedly minor) use of Marc Connelly's 1930 play, *The green pastures*. This is "an idealized version of Old Testament history as seen through the eyes of a small black community in Louisiana" (*FWC* 4, p.56). While only scant use was made of the material, it does help to elucidate some puzzling elements in II.1, the "twilight games" episode. Deane's version, which contains concisely all of the relevant information that we need to record, is repeated below. I omit his salient prefatory remarks and I have made a few corrections, principally of dates. The index was inscribed in the notebook in the early spring of 1931 when Joyce, too depressed to do any real compositional work, passed the time researching angels and devils.

N41 (VI.B.33)

[Draft usage: *black*-deleted material appears in II.1§2.1+ (retyped pages of the first typescript; 1932); *blue*-deleted material appears in II.1§2.2I- (extradraft sheets for the same section, probably late 1932); and, *orange*-deleted material appears in III.3A.10 (pages of *transition* revised in 1933).]

007 —
   (a) trainsgressor
     GP 5/22: Yo' wanter grow up an' be a transgressor?
   (b) on count of
     GP 5/22: Dey wasn't nobody in N'Orleans on count
         dey wasn't any N'Orleans.

(c) mammy angel
   GP 10/25: MAMMY ANGEL
(d) sister
   GP 12/26: De trouble wid you, sister, is you jest got
               minny fishin' on de brain.
(e) ᵇsinbook
   GP 13/27: You wanter be put down in de sin book?
   FW 229.32 47477-84 *JJA51*:145
   II.1§2.2l-
(f) slender angel
   GP 13/27: SLENDER ANGEL

008 —
(a) lardy angel
   GP 13/27: STOUT ANGEL
(b) ᵇᵏwingweary
   GP 16/28: Nowadays Heaven's free of sin an' if a lady
               wants a little constitutional she kin fly 'til
               she wing-weary widout gittin' insulted.
   FW 232.29 47477-62 *JJA51*:059
   II.1§2.1+
(c) the big Boss
   GP 17/29: Now who de big boss?
(d) ᵇᵏcertainly, Lode
   GP 19/30: Certainly, Lawd.
   FW 232.23 47477-62 *JJA51*:059
   II.1§2.1+
(e) ᵇᵏDo you bow mighty low?
   GP 20/31: Do you bow mighty low?
   FW 232.22 47477-62 *JJA51*:059
   II.1§2.1+

(f) <f> fermanent
   GP 24/33: It [the custard] needs jest a little bit mo'
         firmament.

009 —
   (a) rear back & pass a miracle
      GP 25/33: I'll jest r'ar back an' pass a miracle.
   (b) plenty too / much
      GP 25/33: Dat's *plenty* too much firmament.
   (c) ^{bk}is you?
      GP 27/35: You ain't going to let dat go to waste is you,
            Lawd?
      FW 232.21 47477-62 *JJA51*:059
      II.1§2.1+
   (d) field hand
      GP 30/36: [ADAM] *dressed in the clothing of the*
            average field hand
   (e) enjoy yourself
      GP 30/36: [ADAM] *almost laughs in his enjoyment*

010 —
   (a) wars I you,
      GP 38/40: But I do say was I you I'd jest git myself
            down de road
   (b) a trusting male
      GP 39/41: Knock me down for a trustin' baby!
   (c) tooken
      GP 39/41: If I thought you was tryin' to mash me, I'd
            call de police an' git you tooken in de first
            precinct.
   (d) °cooling myself in the element

> *GP* 40/42: CAIN: What was you doin' in dat tree?
> CAIN'S GIRL: Jest coolin' myself in de
> element.
> *FW* 526.31 47486a-111 *JJA61*:083
> III§3A.10
> (e) beautiful
> *GP* 41/42: Where you boun' for, Beautiful?

One should note that whereas the phrase "plenty too much" appears in the index above, it is not tied to the text of *Finnegans wake* despite the similar "plenty good enough" at 311.35. The latter derives from a *Huckleberry Finn* index in N53 (VI.B.46), the unit most aboriginally coming from "The duke's room was pretty small, but plenty good enough, and so was my cubby" (*HF*, chapter 26).

A charge which may perhaps be levelled against genetic exegesis of this sort is that the meaning of the units in the text can be understood without reference to the notebooks or to sources; for example, a reader might well already know that Uatch amulets were commonly made of mother-of-emerald and the use to which they were put. This is fair enough; every reader will of course understand without assistance a number of the references (the inside jokes, to put it another way) in this encyclopaedic work. But different readers will know different things and it is surely an objective of the scholarly enterprise to be comprehensive. Secondly, by *restricting* (in the work of exegesis) the meaning of a unit to that which it originally carried we can avoid an anarchic and ultimately meaningless proliferation of interpretations. Individual readers are, of course, entitled to read into anything anything that they like; it is a free country. Idiosyncratic interpretations, however, can never attain the heuristic status of verifiable objective historical facts. I am aware, I should add, of the "theoretical" arguments against the very concept of objectivity bandied about nowadays. While these arguments do contain an ounce of sense, they also contain a ton of nonsense. Finally, it is solely through the index connection that we can analyse the larger patterns of Joyce's work in progress.

In a great many instances, furthermore, the meanings of the elements Joyce used *are* arcane and could not reasonably be known to even the most erudite and insomniac of ideal readers. For example, what can one unaided make of the first footnote on p.275 — "A pengeneepy for your warcheekeepy"? Or of "a wheeze we has ... jisty and pithy af durck rosolun" (351.07ff.) — *jisty*? *pithy*? Or, indeed, what is the meaning of the transparent but mysterious paragraph with which Joyce ends the third part of the book: "Tiers, tiers and tiers. Rounds."

The first of the above derives from an index in VI.C.2, whose source, Otto Jespersen's *Language: its nature, development and origin* (London: Allen and Unwin, 1922), was identified by Roland McHugh. Jespersen writes (p.150): "'Ziph' or 'Hypernese' (at Winchester) substitutes *wa* for the first of two initial consonants and inserts *p* or *g*, making 'breeches' into *wareechepes* and 'penny' into *pegennepy*." "Jisty" and "pithy" can be found in N53 (VI.B.46) in a Ruthenian language index (who could have guessed it?): the words are verbs, meaning to eat and to drink, respectively. As for the exquisitely balanced end of III.4, while it may seem to reflect the global structure of *Finnegans wake* with its cyclicity and its Viconian helix, reference to its source, W.G. Fay's *Short glossary of theatrical terms* (London: Samuel French, 1930), indexed in N51 (VI.B.44), reveals it to be a picture of the end of a theatrical performance: "tiers" being the term for the rows of seats in the various circles in the theatre and "rounds" denoting "the applause given by the audience". That we have been watching *a play* in III.4 comes as a complete and delicious surprise!

One could go on all night citing increasingly more esoteric identifications possible only through notebook analysis, but I think the point is adequately made.

15 *How Joyce planted* The trees of Ireland *in* Finnegans wake

> To conclude purely negatively from the positive absence of political odia and monetary requests that its page cannot ever have been a penproduct of a man or woman of that period or those parts is only one more unlookedfor conclusion leaped at, being tantamount to inferring from the nonpresence of inverted commas (sometimes called quotation marks) on any page that its author was always constitutionally incapable of misappropriating the spoken words of others. (*FW* 108)

I should like in this chapter to illustrate, briefly but adequately, the manner in which Joyce derived and re-assembled the elements which create the textual compositum of *Finnegans wake*. The "narrative" — the macrocosm of the work viewed as a whole as distinct from the microcosm of the individual parts — has been considered in earlier chapters. I want here to look at how Joyce applied the paint, so to speak, to the canvas, while acknowledging that the pigments used by an artist are not the painting, though the painting cannot exist without them. *In nuce*, the sense of the wor(l)d must necessarily lie outside the wor(l)d. As he himself put it:

> Who in his heart doubts either that the facts of feminine clothiering are there all the time or that the feminine fiction,

stranger than the facts, is there also at the same time, only a little to the rere? Or that one may be separated from the other? Or that both may then be contemplated simultaneously? Or that each may be taken up and considered in turn apart from the other? (*FW*, 109)

On 10 July 1934, Joyce wrote to Harriet Weaver:

Léon began to read to me from a scientific publication about Irish trees. The first sentence was to the effect that the oldest tree in the island is the elm tree in the demesne of Howth Castle and Environs (*Letters III* 308f.)

In March 1993, I wrote to Antony Farrell of the Lilliput Press, who had lately published a *de luxe* edition of a study of Irish trees, and asked him if he could contact the author to see if he could perhaps identify for me this "scientific publication". Within days I was referred to "Fitzpatrick, H.M. 1933. The trees of Ireland — native and introduced. *Scientific proceedings of the Royal Dublin Society 20* (41): 597-656", on the first page (not sentence) of which I read:

Little is known regarding the early introduction of exotic species. According to Loudon the oldest introduced tree in Ireland is an English Elm still standing at Howth Castle, which, he states, was planted about 1585. A painting of the castle and grounds, said by Mr. Gaisford St. Lawrence to have been done in the reign of Queen Anne, certainly shows this elm as a large tree, with the formal beech hedges, which were so fashionable in gardens at the commencement of the eighteenth century, scarcely six feet high beside it.

Searching in the forest of the notebooks for a Tree Index, as Joyce seemed psychologically incapable of passing over anything that interested him without taking from it, and knowing the exact date of his reading of the material, I was led to N46, pages 206-208. This affords us our first Tree Index:

N46 (VI.B.36):206 –

(b) horsechestnut \

> *Fitzpatrick* 599: Weymouth Pine at Adare, Horsechestnuts at Mount Usher, and Balsam Poplars at Ballybeg, Co. Kildare, are recorded by Wakefield in his "Survey of Ireland" in 1812.

(c) elm \ [See above *re* Howth Castle]

(d) yews \

> *Fitzpatrick* 597: The Yew was probably the only tree planted in Ireland up to the end of the Middle Ages.

(e) wehmouth pine ´ Balsam Popalar [sic] \ [see unit (b) above]

N46:207 –

(a) & the 5 cedars of Mt Anville soughing syrially to his obeisance \

> *Fitzpatrick* 613: *Cedrus Libani* Loudon (*C. libanotica*, Trew). Occurring in the mountains of Syria and Asia

Minor the Lebanon Cedar reaches an immense size in its
native home and thrives remarkably in Ireland ... There
are five fine trees at Mount Anville, Dundrum, Co.
Dublin ... said to be the oldest in Ireland.

(b) by Juniper \ *Fitzpatrick* 617 describes *Juniperus*

(c) cupress \ *Fitzpatrick* 614 describes *Cupressus*

(d) <lari> larix o'tourist whetawhistling in astuntedness ˝
& tamboys a beeches tittertattering his tendronym \

Fitzpatrick 619 describes *Larix*: ... These larches have
stout, spreading, weeping branches ... At Lucan House
there is an old tree with a broken stem and a girth of
about 13' which has probably the same origin as the
Doneraile trees.

The reading was curtailed at this point. Perhaps Madame
Léon came in with the tea. Or they had more pressing
business to conduct; Joyce had come back from Dieppe the
previous day and was about to quit his flat and leave for a
five-month stay in Switzerland. Hang on to that article, he
might have said, I will get back to it. And he did, some three
and a half years later, in the first week of February 1938,
when he entered into N53 (VI.B.46) a longer and much more
important index. In my edition of that notebook, *The index
manuscript*, I edited the index as well as I taxonomically
could in default of the sourcetext but, more significantly, I
posited for analytical reasons a *missing* manuscript leaf
containing the first half of the index (which absent leaf I also
duly edited). In a neat demonstration of the scientific

verifiability of notebook exegesis, the unearthing of Fitzpatrick's scientific publication confirms the accuracy in this and expands on my commentary, adding at the same stroke the global detail that the trees in the *Wake*, common native and foreign exotic — with the possible exception of the mahoganies — were all real trees grown in Ireland. In passing, one notes that Joyce seems to have misunderstood a hypsometer to be a species of tree and *athrotaxis* to be a strain of disease. Placenames, also, were slightly less than perfectly reproduced. The units, which were added at galley stage, appear in *Finnegans wake* in four contexts:

(1) In I.4, *FW* 100 — in conjunction with material from an O'Reilly index (from the *Weekly Irish Times*) also in N53 — where rumours of HCE's continued existence are bolstered by signs of life in his house:

> aslike as asnake comes sliduant down that oaktree onto the duke of beavers (you may have seen some liquidamber exude exotic from a balsam poplar at Parteen-a-lax, Limestone Road, and cried Abies Magnifica! not, noble fir?)

(2) In I.6, *FW* 159f, as a learned aside thrown in by the erudite Professor Jones (Shaun).

> (The meeting of mahoganies, be the waves, rementions me that this exposed sight though it pines for an umbrella of its own and needs a shelter belt of the true service sort to keep its boles clean — the weeping beeches, Picea and Tillia, are in a wild state about it — ought to be classified, as Cricketbutt Willowm and his two nurserymen advisers suggested, under genus Inexhaustible when we refloat upon all the butternut, sweet

gum and manna ash redcedera which is so purvulent there as if
there was howthorns in Curraghchasa which ought to look as
plane as a lodgepole to anybody until we are introduced to that
pinetacotta of Verney Rubens where the deodarty is pinctured
for us in a pure stand, which we do not doubt he has a habitat
of doing, but without those selfsownseedlings which are a
species of proof that the largest individual *can* occur at or in an
olivetion such as East Conna Hillock where it mixes with false
accacians and common sallies and *is* tender.) *Vux populus*, as
we say in hickoryhockery and I wish we had some more glasses
of *arbor vitae*. Why root by the roadside or awn over alum pot?
Alderman Whitebeam is oaky-o.

(3) In II.1, *FW* 235, where Issy describes her ideal future
married life with Shaun at La Roseraie, Ailsbury Road:

> Luccombe oaks, Turkish hazels, Greek firs, incense yews
> edcedras. The hypsometers of Mount Anville is held to be
> dying out of arthataxis but, praise send Larix U'Thule, the
> wych elm of Manelagh is still flourishing in the open because
> it's native of our nature and the seeds was sent by Fortune.

(4) Also in II.1, *FW* 246, where Jeremy (Shem), post-
reintroduced after the Zoo Snores piece, is described as "the
chastenot coulter".

The above extracts (find the trees!) are reasonably self-
explanatory (though where is the ALP- and HCE-tropic
Parteen-a-lax or East Conna Hill and what are they doing
here?) but they become even more transparent with reference
to Fitzpatrick. The pertinent, second, more extensive Tree
index follows.

For permission to publish this material — which, as said
above, derives from H. M. Fitzpatrick's *The trees of Ireland*
— I am grateful to the Royal Dublin Society.

N53 (VI.B.46): (*missing leaf* following p.120, reconstituted
contents: these units were almost certainly crossed through
in orange crayon in the lost original) —

(a) species \
Fitzpatrick 597 [Introduction]: The mildness of the Irish
climate makes possible the cultivation of a wide range of
tree species. | [see] *FW* (2) [above]

(b) introduced \
Fitzpatrick 597: the oldest introduced tree in Ireland is an
English Elm | *FW* (2)

(c) Oak \
Fitzpatrick 597: The next [oldest] foreign trees recorded
are a Sycamore ... and an Evergreen Oak growing at
Courtown on the Wexford coast | *FW* (2)

(d) exotics \
Fitzpatrick 597: At Moira, Co. Down, a number of
exotics were planted at about this time by Sir Arthur
Rawdon as the result of a visit to a friend's garden in
England | *FW* (1)

(e) Turkish Hazel \
Fitzpatrick 598: Robinson founded a nursery in Kilkenny
in 1765, and introduced the Turkish Hazel | *FW* (3)

(f) Lucombe Oak \
Fitzpatrick 598: [John Foster] appears to have been the introducer of *Acer rubrum* ... Lucombe Oak ... and American Larch I *FW* (3)

(g) Liquidamber \
Fitzpatrick 598: Templeton introduced ... Canadian Maple, and Liquidamber I *FW* (1)

(h) Horse-chestnuts \
Fitzpatrick 598f: Tighe, in the Survey of Kilkenny, refers to a Cork Oak which in 1801 was 5'1" in girth at ground level, and to a Beech which in 1790 was 24' in girth at 3', and to large Limes, Horse-chestnuts and Planes I *FW* (4)

(i) Balsam Poplar \
Fitzpatrick 599: Balsam Poplars at Ballybeg, Co. Kildare [are recorded by Wakefield, 1812] I *FW* (1)

(j) pineta \
Fitzpatrick 599: After 1840 conifers became the fashion. Their popularity was increased by the discovery of the western North American species, which thrive so remarkably in our climate, and many pineta were established I *FW* (2)

(k) hypsometer \
Fitzpatrick 599: All the tree heights recorded by Mr. Pack-Beresford and by me were measured by means of the geometrical hypsometer (Weise's pattern) made by Wilhelm Göhlers Wittwe, Freiberg-in-Saxony I *FW* (3)

(l) limestone \
  Fitzpatrick 601 ["Places Recorded"]: Adare Manor,
  Adare, Co. Limerick. The Earl of Dunraven. Deep
  limestone drift soil; moderately sheltered; inland I *FW* (1)

(m) shelter belt \
  Fitzpatrick 602: Fota, Co. Cork ... Situated on an island
  in Cork Harbour — a district noted for its mildness; speci-
  men trees protected up to a certain height by shelter belts;
  soil is a reddish brown loam overlying limestone I *FW* (1)

(n) Parteen-a-lax ' limestone \
  Fitzpatrick 604: Parteen-a-lax, Co. Clare. Miss Gwynn.
  Deep limestone soil; moderately exposed; inland I *FW* (1)

(o) native \
  Fitzpatrick 605: [Part II.-Catalogue of Conifers] *Abies
  alba* ... Common Silver Fir. A native of the mountains of
  central and southern Europe, this species was introduced
  into Ireland early in the eighteenth century, has been
  widely planted, and is now a common tree in woods and
  shelter belts I *FW* (3)

(p) pure stand \
  Fitzpatrick 605: *Abies balsamea* ... is found [in North
  America] in pure stands or mixed with other conifers
  I *FW* (2)

(q) Greek Fir \
  Fitzpatrick 605: *Abies cephalonica* Loudon. Greek Fir. A
  native of the mountains of Greece, this fir was introduced
  in 1824 I *FW* (3)

(r) genus \
Fitzpatrick 607: *Abies grandis* [Giant Fir] ... this tree ... is the most vigorous of the genus I *FW* (2)

(s) Abies magnifica \
Fitzpatrick 608: *Abies magnifica* A. Murray. Red Fir. This tree is a native of the mountains of Oregon and California, and was introduced in 1851 I *FW* (1)

(t) Noble Fir \
Fitzpatrick 608: *Abies nobilis* Lindley. The Noble Fir was discovered by David Douglas on the south side of the Columbia River in 1825 ... There are [in Ireland] many beautiful specimens I *FW* (1)

(u) wild state \
Fitzpatrick 610: *Abies venusta* Koch. This tree has an extremely limited range in the wild state ... It was discovered by Coulter in 1831 I *FW* (2)

(v) Coulter \
Fitzpatrick [see unit (u) above] I *FW* (4)

(w) largest individuals \
Fitzpatrick 611: *Araucaria araucana* ... This Chilian tree, popularly known as 'Monkey Puzzle', inhabits the Cordillera of Chile and nothern Patagonia, where it was discovered in 1780 ... There are splendid avenues of these trees at Powerscourt and Woodstock, the largest individuals being 64' x 7'4" and 61' x 6'5" respectively I *FW* (2)

(x) Athrotaxis \
Fitzpatrick 611: *Athrotaxis laxifolia* Hooker. This species has a habitat similar to *A. cupressoides* and is tender. There is a specimen at Kilmacurragh 39' 6" high | *FW* (3)

(y) habitat \
Fitzpatrick [see unit (x) above] | *FW* (2)

(z) is tender \
Fitzpatrick [see unit (x) above] | *FW* (2)

(aa) flourishing \
Fitzpatrick 612: *Callitris oblonga* Richard. The Cypress Pine is a native of Tasmania, where it is found on the banks of the S. Esk and the St. Anne rivers. There is at Rossdohan in Co. Kerry a fine tree 32' high ... This specimen is growing in a well-sheltered spot within 200 yards of the Kenmare River estuary, and was flourishing and bearing numerous cones when seen in 1932 | *FW* (2)

(bb) in the open \
Fitzpatrick 612: *Callitris robusta* R. Brown. This is the common Cypress Pine of Western Australia ... The only specimen known out of doors in Ireland is at Headfort where there is a plant 6'6" high which has survived two winters in the open | *FW* (2)

(cc) Deodar \
Fitzpatrick 612: *Cedrus Deodara* Loudon. The Deodar is an important timber tree in the western Himalayas, reaching its greatest development in the inner valleys

with heavy winter rainfall. It was introduced about 1831, and grows to a large size in this country | *FW* (2)

(dd) Mount Anville \
Fitzpatrick 613: *Cedrus Libani* ... Occurring in the mountains of Syria and Asia Minor the Lebanon Cedar reaches an immense size in its native home ... [It] is now [in Ireland] a rare tree. There are five fine trees at Mount Anville, Dundrum, Co. Dublin, which are said by Loudon to have been brought direct from Lebanon by an ancestor of Lord Tremblestown, and to be the oldest in Ireland. | *FW* (3)

(ee) seed sent by Fortune \
Fitzpatrick 613: *Cryptomeria japonica* D. Don. This species occurs in China and Japan, and is an important tree in the latter country where it is valued for timber and ornament. It was introduced in 1842, and seed in quantity was sent by Fortune in 1844 | *FW* (3)

(ff) selfsown seedling \
Fitzpatrick 615: *Cupressus macrocarpa* Hartweg. The Monterey Cypress ... Introduced about 1838 ... Specimens have been measured at ... Muckross 52' x 2'11", with self-sown seedlings beneath | *FW* (2)

(gg) occurs ' elevation \
Fitzpatrick 616: *Cupressus nootkatensis* Don. The Sitka or Yellow Cypress ... In its southern range it occurs mostly between 2,000 and 5,000 feet elevation ... It was introduced about 1854 and ... is most successful in this country | *FW* (2)

(hh) wild state \

Fitzpatrick 617: *Ginkgo biloba* Linnaeus. The Maidenhair Tree is a commonly-planted tree in China, Manchuria, and Korea, and is found in the grounds of Buddhist temples but is said not to occur in the wild state. It was introduced in 1754 I *FW* (2)

(ii) Larix \

Fitzpatrick 619: LARIX [Genus: Larch] I *FW* (3)

(jj) Incense Cedar \

Fitzpatrick 621: *Libocedrus decurrens* Torrey. The Incense Cedar is a native of Oregon and California ... It was introduced by Jeffrey in 1853, has been planted in most pineta, and is often to be seen in gardens I *FW* (3)

(kk) Picea \

Fitzpatrick 621: PICEA [Genus: Spruce] I *FW* (2)

N53 (VI.B.46):121 –

(a) °lodgepole pine \

Fitzpatrick 626: *Pinus cortorta* Douglas. The Lodgepole Pine ... There are few old trees of either form, but in recent years var. *latifolia* has been used extensively for planting high exposed mountain slopes I *FW* (2)

(b) °held to have died out \

Fitzpatrick 630: *Pinus sylvestris* Linnaeus. The Common or Scots Pine ... The native race is held to have died out, however, and all the present trees are very possibly of foreign origin I *FW* (3)

(c) °alum pot \
{not located in *Fitzpatrick*} | *FW* (2)

(d) °variety \
Fitzpatrick 632: *Podocarpus Totara* ... The Totara is a
timber tree in New Zealand ... Var. *Hallii* Pilger. This
variety is occasionally grown as a shrub in gardens | *FW* (2)

(e) °exposed site \
Fitzpatrick 633: *Pseudotsuga taxifolia* ... The Oregon
Douglas Fir ... has been found to dislike lime in the soil,
and will not grow in exposed situations. There are many
fine trees in Ireland | *FW* (2)

(f) °pine umbrella \
Fitzpatrick 633: *Sciadopitys verticillata* Siebold and
Zuccarini. This tree, known as the Umbrella Pine on
account of the arrangement of its modified branchlets, is
a native of Japan, and was introduced by John Gould
Veitch in 1861 | *FW* (2)

(g) °East Conna Hillock \
Fitzpatrick 634: *Sequoia sempervirens* Endlicher. The
Redwood ... Good specimens are at ... Old Conna Hill 70'
| *FW* (2)

(h) °clean bole \
Fitzpatrick 635: *Taxus baccata* Linnaeus. The Common
Yew is widespread in the northern hemisphere. It is
indigenous to Ireland, but, according to Praeger, is now
of rare occurence in the wild state ... Yew trees are a
feature in many of the old established demesnes such as

Muckross, Castlemartyr 54' x 7'11" with a clean bole to 20' I *FW* (2)

(i) °timber tree \
Fitzpatrick 635: *Tetraclinis articulata* Masters. This is a useful timber tree in Algeria ... There are specimens at Rostrevor 14' I *FW* (3)

(j) °I yew \
Fitzpatrick 635: *Taxus baccata* var. *fastigiata*. This upright form known as the Irish Yew originated about 1780 as a chance seedling, or sport I *FW* (3)

(k) °redcedar
Fitzpatrick 636: *Thuja plicata* ... The Western Red Cedar or Arbor vitae is a native of the Pacific Coast region of North America ... It is a very large tree, and is important for timber ... It grows freely in Ireland, especially on the plains of limestone drift soil I *FW* (2) and (3)

(l) °arbor vitae \
Fitzpatrick [see unit (k) above] I *FW* (2)

(m) °roadside \
Fitzpatrick 640: *Aesculus carnea* Hayne. The Red Horse-chestnut is a hybrid between the Common Horse-chestnut and *A. Pavia*. It is remarkable for its red flowers, and is occasionally seen in parks and gardens and planted as a roadside tree I *FW* (2)

(n) alderman \
Fitzpatrick 640: *Alnus glutinosa* Gaertner. The Common
Alder has a wide distribution ... The Alder is usually a
small tree | *FW* (2)

(o) °tree of heaven \
Fitzpatrick 640: *Ailanthus glandulosa* Desfontaines. The
'Tree of Heaven' is a native of northern China. It was in-
troduced ... into a nursery owned by Robertson at Kil-
kenny in 1765. It is rare in cultivation | [unlocated in *FW*]

(p) °hickory \
Fitzpatrick 642: *Carya alba* Nuttall. A native of the
eastern and southern United States, this Hickory was
introduced in 1629 | *FW* (2)

(q) °nurseryman \
Fitzpatrick 643: *Corylus Colurna* Linnaeus. The Turkish
Hazel has a wide distribution ... Introduced into Ireland
about [1765] when a tree was planted by Robertson, a
nurseryman at Kilkenny | *FW* (2)

(r) °hawth \
Fitzpatrick 643: *Crataegus monogyna* Jacquin. This is
the common native hawthorn in Ireland | *FW* (2)

(s) °weeping beech
Fitzpatrick 646: *Fagus sylvatica* Linnaeus. The Common
Beech ... is not indigenous to Ireland but was introduced,
probably at the end of the seventeenth century ... Var.
pendula Loddiges. There are beautiful examples of the
Weeping Beech at Curraghchase and Rostrevor | *FW* (2)

(t) °Curraghchase \
Fitzpatrick [see unit (s) above] I *FW* (2)

(u) °manna ash \
Fitzpatrick 646: *Fraxinus Ornus* Linnaeus. The Flowering
or Manna Ash ... was introduced about 1710 I *FW* (2)

(v) °butternut \
Fitzpatrick 647: *Juglans cinerea* Linnaeus. The Butternut
is a native of eastern North America and was introduced
about 1656 I *FW* (2)

(w) °sweet gum \
Fitzpatrick 648: *Liquidamber styraciflua* Linnaeus. The
Sweet Gum is distributed in eastern North America ... and
was first cultivated in 1681 by Bishop Compton I *FW* (2)

(x) °3 planes \
Fitzpatrick 649: *Platanus acerifolia* Willdenow. The
London Plane, which is a hybrid between *P. orientalis*
and *P. occidentalis*, is by far the commonest of the three
planes in cultivation I *FW* (2)

(y) °populus \
Fitzpatrick 650: POPULUS [Genus: Poplar] I *FW* (2)

(z) °vernirubens \
Fitzpatrick 651: *Populus vernirubens* A. Henry. This is a
chance hybrid which arose at the time when *P. generosa*
was artifically produced. The female parent is *P. angulata*
but the male parent is unkown. It grows with great vigour,
and is remarkable for its brilliant red leaves in early

summer. The original tree is growing in a garden in Ranelagh, Co. Dublin | *FW* (2)

(aa) tremula \
Fitzpatrick 651: *Populus tremula* Linnaeus. The Common Aspen ... In Ireland it occurs wild in all parts of the country

(bb) °Ranelagh \
Fitzpatrick [see unit (z) above] | *FW* (3)

(cc) aspen \
Fitzpatrick [see unit (aa) above]

(dd) gean \
Fitzpatrick 651: *Prunus Avium* Linnaeus. The Wild Cherry, or Gean, is distributed throughout the whole of Europe

(ee) laurel \
Fitzpatrick 651: *Prunus laurocerasus* Linnaeus. The Common Laurel ... is very common in Ireland as a shrub, but occasionally attains the dimensions of a tree

(ff) °true (wild) service \
Fitzpatrick 652: *Pyrus Sorbus* Gaertner. The True Service ... is occasionally seen in gardens ... *Pyrus torminalis* Ehrhart. The Wild Service ... is a rare tree in cultivation | *FW* (2)

(gg) °whitebeam \
Fitzpatrick 652: *Pyrus Aria* Ehrhart. The Whitebeam ...

occurs wild in Ireland. It is rare and local as a wild tree and is seldom seen planted I *FW* (2)

(hh) °false acacias \
Fitzpatrick 654: *Robinia pseudoacacia* Linnaeus. The False Acacia ... appears to have been first planted in Ireland at Cypress Grove near Dublin by the Earl of Clanbrassil between 1770 and 1790, and was at one time a fairly common tree. It is now occasionally seen in old gardens I *FW* (2)

(ii) °common sallies \
Fitzpatrick 654: *Salix Caprea* Linnaeus. The Common Sallow is a native of Ireland, it is found growing in woods on wet ground or near streams I *FW* (2)

(jj) °Cricketbutt Willowm \
Fitzpatrick 654: *Salix cocrulea* Smith. The Cricket-bat Willow is a tree of obscure origin, and is possibly a hybrid ... There is a small tree in Glasnevin I *FW* (2)

(kk) Tillia \
Fitzpatrick 655: TILIA [Genus: Lime] I *FW* (2)

(ll) f. parent \
Fitzpatrick 651: The female parent ...

(mm) wych elm \

Fitzpatrick 656: *Ulmus montana* Stokes. The Mountain or Wych Elm is a native of Ireland, and is a common tree in hedges in most parts of the country I *FW* (3)

16 The Raphael transcriptions: "flexionals" into "fleas and snails"

Late in 1933, Madame France Raphael, a Parisienne, began work as James Joyce's amanuensis. It was her task to prepare for him clean, readable transcriptions of the uncrossed and therefore unused entries in those primary, authorially inscribed notebooks given to her. Joyce was lately back from Switzerland and he had amassed well over forty primary notebooks: too many to handle conveniently and, besides, he complained that he was unable to read his own handwriting. They were indeed very nearly illegible. It should therefore come as no surprise that Madame Raphael made many mistakes in her transcriptions, and skipped over the odd page or two.[1] In addition, not knowing or knowing only very imperfectly the sense of what she was transcribing, the cohesion of individual elements was often disrupted by her intervention. Joyce nevertheless did make use of these copies in much the same way as, but less heavily than, he did with the originals. When a notebook was copied and returned (take note!) the original was never again referred to or used

[1] Transcriptions were made of 37 of the 44 notebooks compiled by late 1933. Of the 7 not copied, N4 (VI.B.25) had already been (partly) transcribed into SD1 in early 1931; N3 (VI.B.3) and N29 (VI.B.21) had effectively been exhausted (transcribed onto worksheets) by Joyce in the summer of 1933; and, finally, N3 (VI.X.1), N7 (VI.X.2), N27 (VI.X.3) and N39 (VI.X.4) had either by Raphael's time become lost or had been (possibly partly) transcribed into SA, SD1 or into worksheets.

in any way. Raphael's work continued off and on until January or February 1937.[1]

In the present chapter — a brief glance at one of these transcriptions, the first (VI.C.1) — I wish to put into focus Joyce's practice during this phase of the composition of *Finnegans wake*. In passing, I shall also illustrate the several possible routes which the ingredient elements of his book followed in the course of their assimilation into the final text. This route, as we shall see, was not invariably source → notebook → draft → final text. At one level it even entailed a creation *ex nihilo*. Even here, however, we can exclude Joyce's knowing involvement. Our clarification of this last point should prove of some considerable concern to those who struggle to oppose what they view as the usurpation of the Creator Joyce by Joyce the Assembler.

To begin, it has been established that Joyce used the notebooks, primary and secondary, as the source for the textual elements that collectively comprise the text of *Finnegans wake*. We also know that these elements did not originate with Joyce but were imported ready-made and derive from external sources. We thus identify a process of composition entailing a preparatory process of compilation, as follows:

multiple sources

↓

notebook (in distillation)

↓

---

[1]   Of the six notebooks (N45-N50) compiled by Joyce during the period of the transcriptions, only two were copied by Madame Raphael. These two — N48(VI.B.38) and N50(VI.B.37) — were the very last to be transcribed.

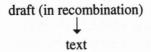

draft (in recombination)
↓
text

This is the general case, the setting-forth on its journey by a word or phrase being indicated for the most part (but not invariably) by Joyce's crossing through of the departing guest with a child's crayon. On the other hand, those many elements that were collected by Joyce and housed in the notebooks, but never subsequently used by him, had the rather shorter journey of:

source → notebook [terminus].

The basic situation outlined above is complicated slightly by the inclusion of the Raphael transcriptions, as we must now interpose a new factor. The new textual line in these cases is:

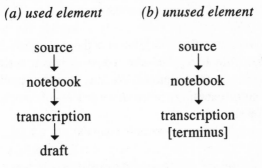

(a) used element   *(b) unused element*

source   source
↓   ↓
notebook   notebook
↓   ↓
transcription   transcription
↓   [terminus]
draft

One would be hasty to assume that, in the case of the transcriptions, this is it, that there are no more loops. In the not untypical case of VI.C.1, for example, the majority of the crossed units were not transferred directly to the drafts, but instead first made their way (in a patterned manner which is outside the scope of this purview) onto extradraft manuscript

pages or worksheets (the Sheets), a kind of halfway house.
Only thence, in their altered environment (their third such
metamorphosis) did they enter into the drafts proper. Unless
the transferral terminated on a worksheet (which it did
occasionally), the full line, accordingly, is :

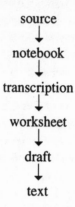

It is reasonable to ask what happened to the units, given all
this shuffling along. To what degree did these wandering
jews still resemble their original selves when finally they
came home to rest?[1]

In an ideal world, Madame Raphael would have accurately
transcribed into her copy all of the unused material in the
source notebooks. This did not happen, of course; errors of
transmission and omission arose in all possible ways. Pages
were skipped; thus, for example, pp.72-3 and 88-9 of N10
(VI.B.16) were never transcribed into VI.C.1, impossibilizing
the inclusion in the work in progress of any of their ingredient

---

[1]   A small number of the VI.C.1 elements escaped the worksheets and,
unless some of these sheets are lost, were transferred directly into the work
in progress.

elements. One of these is the delightful "tinkers' asses tied to memorial". More commonly, whenever she faced a word too illegible for her to decipher she simply omitted it but did not indicate the lacuna in her transcription. For many elements this exclusion renders the underlying sense of what was transcribed meaningless. To crown it all, she rarely transcribed elements in their original coherence, unit by unit; instead, pedantically, she copied the entries line by line. Where a mistranscription occurred in one such line fragment its connection with the rest of itself, as it were, was often lost, creating in its train two problems: the automatic loss of the sense of the original element and the creation of misleading pseudo-elements by virtue of the copyist's intervention. An example of the latter appears on VI.C.1:141, where Madame Raphael wrote the following two lines:

> rightcheek disciple
> injured £40.000

When he read this, Joyce attempted, as he invariably did, to reconstruct the original sense. In this case, however, he failed to realize that the two units were originally one. Thinking, perhaps, of the notion of a chap's turning the other cheek by way of passive response, he transferred the unit to a worksheet (MS 474786a-7, *JJA61*:122) as "right cheek discipline" and subsequently used this invention (false correction) on draft III§1A.12/1B.3 (MS 47486a-74v, *JJA61*:8) where it ultimately became *FW* 411.12ff: "I am awful good ... praised be right cheek Discipline!" Notwithstanding Shaun's admirable Christianity, it is regrettable that the original reading "rightcheek dimple insured for £40,000" was lost in the process of transcription. Issy, if not

Shaun, could have done with that precious dimple. A second example appears on VI.C.1:256 :

> answers with
> before letter

Assuming that "before letter" actually meant something on its own, yesterday's letter perhaps, Joyce transferred it to sheet 47486a-7v (*JJA61*:123) and thence to draft III.1D.12 (MS 474786a-78; *JJA61*:20) whence it became *FW* 421.24f: "Notorious I rather would feel inclined to myself in the first place to describe Mr O' Shem the Draper with before letter as should I be accentually called upon ... to pass my opinions". What can "with before letter" mean here? In its original form the element read "answers written before letter", altogether a different kettle of fish.

In very many cases, naturally, Madame Raphael accurately transcribed the unit and Joyce retransferred it in its correct form into the drafts, losing and creating nothing in the process. Even here, however, one must ask, To what degree did the original *context* of the element remain known or knowable to him? Did it matter? There can be no doubt that when working with the primary notebooks Joyce was aware of both the sense and context of the material he was importing into his text. But when dealing with a partial, and partly garbled, transcription made many years after the original compilation, it is not reasonable to assume that Joyce always retained a comprehensive sense of the contextual significance of the individual units. Sometimes he did and sometimes he didn't. In most cases the evidence shows that he was responding to the reduced, immediate sense of the fragments. This is of crucial significance in our attempts to delineate his attentions, at least in the post-Raphael period. That he sought to restore the lost sense of manifestly defective elements is evidenced in scores of examples. Let us consider a few from the notebook in question.

> *original reading*: "love thro' the usual channels"
> *copied form*: "live this the usual channels" (VI.C.1:262)
> *sheet form*: "love thro usual channels" (*JJA61*:158)
> *text*: "(Love through the usual channels, cisternbrothelly ...)", *FW* 436.14, relevant element entered *JJA61*:30, at draft III§2A.13/2B.11/2C.13.

or, more telling yet:

> *original reading*: "I'd love a dress of that, Eve to Satan"
> *copied form*: "I'd love a day of that Eve td Satan" (VI.C.1:173)
> *sheet form*: "and the downslider in that snakes to naughsy ^[whispering] whimering^ woman't she leib a satan dress of that" (*JJA61*:169)
> *text*: "and her downslyder in that snakedst-tu-naughsy whimmering woman't seeleib such a fashionaping sathinous dress out of that exquisite creation", *FW* 505.07f, relevant element entered *JJA61*:70, at draft III§3A.10.

Some of Madame Raphael's inventions are exotic creatures whose protoypes could not be guessed at by even the most inspired of reconstructionists. What, for example, could be the original form of "humping in at 1d" (VI.C.1:92)? Small wonder Joyce skipped over it. Yet the original is the comical "humping Matilda" which, had he been aware of it, he might well have used. Or consider Raphael's "glyc and fbckamal" (VI.C.1:214). What in God's name is the original of "fbckamal"? Could it be "becalmed", or "caramel"? Joyce passed it over, for the unlikely solution is "blackcurrant"! "Chrsmt Sunday" (VI.C.1:219) is relatively easy — "Chestnut Sunday"; but "∧b queer table" (VI.C.1:228) must give pause. This is not particularly interesting or meaningful and Joyce left it alone. However, what it should have read — "∧b green table" — may well have appeared somewhere along the line at one of Shaun's Gargantuan dinners. Some other examples of elements which Joyce, baffled, failed to respond to, are: "Nothing er I was eleven" (VI.C.1:185), "bopidy of corn — 60 p" (VI.C.1:192), "Marriage rglity" (VI.C.1:193), "the graid be splithy smile of ... suffering Grizelda" (VI.C.1:212), "⊣ sills notepaper in sheet after" (VI.C.1:222), "⊣ F amt" (VI.C.1:229), "forestore belief to Crown" (VI.C.1:230), "⊓ hair on child = furse on Hill" (VI.C.1:245), "horrid crowd" (VI.C.1:246), and, "∧ related to 2 j prishon" (VI.C.1:253).[1]

With regard to the mistranscriptions, two possible situations pertain, some instances of which we have already noted above. In the first, Joyce looked at the transcribed unit, appreciated that it was botched beyond recall and gave up (e.g. the indigestible "fbckamal"). In the second, he looked at the unit, realized that there was a problem, corrected it to the best of his ability and transferred into the text what he

[1]   The originals of these nonsense lines are, respectively, "rolling stone since I was eleven", "60 pecks of corn — 60p", "marriage rights", "the granite-splitting smile of ... suffering Grizelda", "⊣ sells notepaper in street after dark", "⊣ T aunt", "foreshore belongs to crown", "⊓ hair on chest = furze on hill", "hoodie crow" and "∧ related to 27 priests & nuns".

assumed was the correct reading, though occasionally making a new mistake in the process. Examples are: "1 to 6 W of same name" (VI.C.1:209) which he transferred as "O woman of same name" (*JJA61*:171), the source for the III.3A.10 draft insertion "I am afraid my poor woman of that same name" (*JJA61*:67, now *FW* 495.35). The original reading is the simple "H & W [husband and wife] of same name". Faced with a curious "bouq" in ""wornout shoes upon his feet / in his hand a bouq" (VI.C.1:186), he decided, with footgear in mind, that this must have been "boot" (though "book" or "bouquet" equally spring to mind) and transferred the phrase to sheet *JJA61*:170 as "wornout shoes upon his feet ... in his hands a boot ...". This entered the text at *FW* 489.22f via draft III.3A.10 (*JJA61*:64). The correct reading is the more poignant "banjo". The poor fellow in the note was originally a musician.

A third situation occurred when Joyce suspected nothing, took Raphael's innocent-looking but erroneous element at face value and transferred it uncorrected into his text. A few examples follow, with (1) = original reading; (2) = Raphael's version; (3) = sheet version; and, (4) = version in the text.

(1) "she hasn't a bit on her"
(2) "she buds and bit on her" (VI.C.1:1)
(3) "would you wait biss she buds ^[to] till you^ bite on her?" (*JJA61*:145)
(4) As above, *FW* 465.10f, via *JJA61*:47, draft III§2A.13/ 2B.11/2C.13.

(1) "colour of hair & voice"
(2) "Colonel if have a voice" (VI.C.1:27)

(3) "he cd be near a colonel with that voice" (*JJA61*:128)

(4) "But he could be near a colonel with a voice like that",
    FW 466.36, via *JJA61*:48, draft III§2A.13/2B.11/
    2C.13.

(1) "gave of his best blood"

(2) "gave of his best door" (VI.C.1:78)

(3) "who gave sup but he gave of his best door"
    (*JJA61*:188)

(4) [unused in *FW*]

(1) "rash act"

(2) "rusty Oct" (VI.C.1:81)

(3) "while it's rusty october in this Bleak Forrest"
    (*JJA61*:122)

(4) "till it's rusty October in this bleak forest", *FW* 410.09,
    via *JJA61*:8, draft III§1A.12/1B.3.

(1) "jeu d'initiation"

(2) "jeu d'inspiration" (VI.C.1:111)

(3) { no worksheet reference }

(4) "Exquisite Game of inspiration!", *FW* 302.19f, via
    JJA53:223, draft II.2§8.12.

(1) "fruitflavoured tea"

(2) "fruitflavoured lip" (VI.C.1:127)

(3) "fruitflavoured lips" (*JJA61*:154)

(4) "I'll smack your fruitflavoured jujube lips well for
    you", *FW* 444.22, via *JJA61*:34, draft III§2A.13/
    2B.11/2C.13.

(1) "Old Tom, best snuff noses had ever run across"
(2) "O to some best snuff noses had over run across"
     (VI.C.1:150)
(3) { unlocated }
(4) { unlocated }

(1) "always with him is the ambition to"
(2) "always with him at the arch tree" (VI.C.1:253)
(3) "who is always with him at the Arch or the Big Elm"
     (*JJA61*:197)
(4) "who is always with him at the Big Elm and the Arch",
     FW 507.36f, via *JJA61*:75, draft III§3A.10

Accordingly, there is for *Finnegans wake* one source which is, was and always will be virtual but which can at the same time be delineated and detailed much as any other: namely, those inventions which Madame France Raphael, straining to read, plucked as it were out of the blue, thereby unknowingly contributing to James Joyce's masterpiece fragments of her very own composition.[1]

In a short paper written some years ago, "Mutant units in the C notebooks" (*FWC* 2, pp.76f.), Ian MacArthur points out the disparity between the originals of seven units in N6 (VI.B.11) and their transcribed versions in VI.C.1. He then comments:

Where do we go from here? Firstly we need a complete listing of mutants: I leave this to someone who has easy access to Archive material. Secondly we need to think

[1] One of her more inspired inventions appears as "Jim's Hotel" on VI.C.1:136. Joyce would of course have instantly recognized this as what it was meant to be: "Finn's Hotel".

about the implications. Some of these are profound and raise questions about the nature of art. Surely this must be a unique compositional method and can certainly be interpreted in both a positive and a negative way. I prefer to concentrate on the former. I suggest that it is one of Joyce's techniques following the commonplace idea that dreams are distortions of everyday life. The notebook units represent such life. At first (during the early stages of composition) Joyce is content to rearrange them. Later he distorts them more and more, making them less easy to recognize. Finally he uses the accidental mistranscriptions.

I disagree with this view on fundamental grounds. The writer is assuming that the notebooks are a part of the draft record. They are not. They belong to a purely compilational phase of the work in progress antecedent to the act of composition. To put it another way: the words were not yet Joyce's until they left the notebook page. The inferences he draws, moreover, are fanciful. I have demonstrated that Joyce did not deliberately transfer distorted material into his text because it was distorted (and "original"). In an earlier chapter I have outlined the efficient cause of Wakean distortion. A close study of his use of the Raphael copies repeatedly confirms, moreover, that as far as the meaning in the final text is concerned, Joyce's main concern was with the immediate common-sense meaning (even though this was not necessarily the original sense) of the elements he incorporated. In contrast to the case of the primary notebooks (from which he derived a great many terms the specialized sense of which is not always apparent), Joyce was not always aware of the context of the transcribed units. It follows that the original source context is less important in these cases. As for the implications for Art, these are not where the writer suggests that we should seek them—in imagined dream representation — but rather in James Joyce's engagement in the cold, premeditated act of appropriation itself.

Acknowledgments

In preparing this book I have benefitted most particularly and invaluably from the research of John O'Hanlon and Vincent Deane who have generously allowed me to use large blocks of their unpublished material. In addition, I should like to thank Geert Lernout and his past and present colleagues at Antwerp (Wim Van Mierlo, Andrew Treip and Ingeborg Landuyt). Otherwise, I am of course in diverse ways indebted to that eminent "schola of tinkers" who in one way or another have through the years worked on the *Finnegans wake* manuscripts: these include Peter Spielberg, Thomas Connolly, Matthew Hodgart, Walt Litz, Fred Higginson, James Atherton, Jack Dalton, David Hayman, Clive Hart, Ian MacArthur, Fritz Senn, Jacques Aubert, Carole and Leo Knuth, Claude Jacquet, Michael Groden, Roland McHugh, Ward Swinson, Petr Skrabanek, Laurent Milesi, Richard Brown, Jorn Barger, Sam Slote, Verej Nersessian, Mikio Fusé, Luigi Schenoni, Daniel Ferrer and Joe Schork. My personal gratitude is extended to Ian Gunn and Alistair McCleery for their supererogatory concern in seeing this book so aesthetically into print. Lastly, for their inspiration, patience and understanding, I must thank Catherine, Jane, Kate, Conor, Aidan, Maureen, Cel, Ken, Shanny, Ludie, Baby, Jack Hart and Pop.

Appendix A: James Joyce's addresses 1922-1941

The following list details all of the addresses at which James Joyce stayed between October 1922, when he began to take notes for a new post-*Ulysses* work, and January 1941, when he died. In preparing this list, I have made use of an earlier chronology prepared by Richard Ellmann (*Letters II* lviii-lxii) and of an important study, *"The Joyce Calendar: a chronological listing of published, unpublished and ungathered correspondence by James Joyce"*, comp. by Richard B. Watson and Randolph Lewis (Austin: *Joyce Studies Annual*, 1994). In addition, I have examined, read through for further internal evidence both published and unpublished correspondence of Joyce and his associates. I have also indicated the dates of some important events which pertain to Joyce's health.

Code: 12 Oct = date; *12 Oct = estimated date (probable);
**12 Oct = estimated date (uncertain): 12/14 Oct = a day on or
    between 12 October and 14 October.

SOUTH OF FRANCE 11/12 OCT → *14 NOV 1922
    Dijon: 11/12 Oct → 12/13 Oct 1922
    Marseille: 12/13 Oct → 13 Oct 1922
    Hôtel de France, Nice: 13 Oct → 14/16 Oct 1922
    Hôtel Suisse, Nice: 14/16 Oct → 12 Nov 1922
        (Dr Louis Colin: leeches on eye)

Le Grand Hotel, Marseille: 12 Nov → 13 Nov 1922
Lyon: 13 Nov → 14 Nov 1922

PARIS: 14 NOV 1922 → 18 JUN 1923
   26 Avenue Charles Floquet: 14 Nov 1922 → 3 Apr 1923
   Maison de Santé Ambroise Paré, Neuilly: 3 Apr → 11/14 Apr 1923
      (Dental Op.: 17 teeth extracted)
   26 Avenue Charles Floquet, Paris: 11/14 Apr → 25 Apr 1923
   Dr Borsch's Clinique, 39 rue du Cherche-Midi: 25 Apr → 2/6
      May 1923
      (Eye Ops. #2, #3 iridectomy and sphincterectomy left eye)
   26 Avenue Charles Floquet, Paris: 2/6 May → 18 Jun 1923

SOUTH OF ENGLAND: 18 JUN → *17 AUG 1923
   Terminus Hotel, Calais: 18 Jun → 21 Jun 1923
   London: 21 Jun → *29 Jun 1923
   Alexandra House, Bognor: *29 Jun → 3 Aug 1923
   Belgrave Residential Hotel, London: 3 Aug → *17 Aug 1923

PARIS: *17 AUG → 27 AUG 1923
   Victoria Palace Hotel: *17 Aug → 27 Aug 1923

TOURS: 27 Aug → *3 Sep 1923
   Hôtel de l'Univers, Tours: 27 Aug → *3 Sep 1923
      S. Patrice: 1 Sep 1923

PARIS: *3 SEP 1923 → 5/10 JUL 1924
   Victoria Palace Hotel, Paris: *3 Sep 1923 → *10 Jun 1924
   Clinique des yeux: *10 Jun → **22 Jun 1924
      (Eye Op. #4 iridectomy left eye: 11 Jun 1924)
   Victoria Palace Hotel: **22 Jun → 5/10 Jul 1924

BRITTANY, FRANCE: 5/10 JUL → *5 SEP 1924
    Hôtel de France et Chateaubriand, Saint-Malo: 5/10 Jul → *18
        Aug 1924
    Hôtel de l'Epée, Quimper: *18 Aug → 28/29 Aug 1924
    Grand Hôtel du Commerce et de l'Épée, Vannes 28/29 Aug →
        *5 Sep 1924
    Carnac: 1 Sep 1924

PARIS: *5 SEP → 15 SEP 1924
    Victoria Palace Hotel: *5 Sep → 15 Sep 1924

LONDON: 15 SEP → *12 OCT 1924
    Hôtel Terminus, Calais: 15 Sep → 18/19 Sep 1924
    Euston Hotel, London: 18/19 Sep → *12 Oct 1924

PARIS: *12 OCT 1924 → 21 JUL 1925
    8 Avenue Charles Floquet: *12 Oct 1924 → *28 Nov 1924
    Clinique des yeux: *28 Nov → **10 Dec 1924
        (Eye Op. #5 (6) Secondary cataract left eye: 29 Nov 1924)
    8 Avenue Charles Floquet: **10 Dec 1924 → *15 Feb 1925
    Clinique des yeux: *15 Feb → 25 Feb 1925
        (Conjunctivitis attack: leeches on eye)
    8 Avenue Charles Floquet: 25 Feb → 15 Apr 1925
    Clinique des yeux: 15 Apr → *25 Apr 1925
        (Eye Op. #6 (7) incomplete capsulotomy left eye: 16 Apr 1925)
    8 Avenue Charles Floquet: *25 Apr → *14 May 1925
    Victoria Palace Hotel: *14 May → *1 Jun 1925
    2 Square Robiac: *1 Jun → 21 Jul 1925

NORTHERN AND WESTERN FRANCE: 21 JUL → 5 SEP 1925
    Grand Hôtel des Bains et de Londres, Fécamp: 21 Jul → 28
        Jul 1925

Grand Hôtel de la Poste, Rouen: 28 Jul → 9 Aug 1925
   Les Andelys: Hôtel du Grand-Cerf: 6 Aug 1925
Grand Hôtel du Raisin de Bourgogne, Niort: 9 Aug → 10 Aug
   1925
Bordeaux: 10 Aug → 11 Aug 1925
Régina Palace Hotel et d'Angleterre, Arcachon: 11 Aug → *3
   Sep 1925
Hotel Bayonne, Bordeaux: *3 Sep → 5 Sep 1925

PARIS: 5 SEP 1925 → *5 AUG 1926
   2 Square Robiac: 5 Sep → *5 Dec 1925
   Clinique des yeux: *5 Dec → 15 Dec 1925
      (Eye Ops. #7 and#8 (8): 5 and 8 Dec 1925)
   2 Square Robiac: 15 Dec 1925 → *5 Aug 1926

BELGIUM: *5 AUG → 29 SEP 1926
   Auberge Littoral Palace, Ostende: *5 Aug → 9 Aug 1926
   Hotel du Phare, Ostende: 9 Aug → 11/18 Aug 1926
   Hotel de l'Océan, Ostende: 11/18 Aug → 13 Sep 1926
   Ghent: 13 Sep → 17 Sep 1926
   Grand Hotel, Anvers (Antwerp): 17 Sep → 20 Sep 1926
   Hôtel Astoria & Claridge, Brussels: 20 Sep → 29 Sep 1926
      Waterloo: 22 Sep 1926

PARIS: 29 SEP 1926→ 4 APR 1927
   2 Square Robiac, Paris: 29 Sep 1926 →4 Apr 1927

LONDON: 4 APR → *8 APR 1927
   Euston Hotel, London: 4 Apr → *8 Apr 1927
      (P.E.N. Club dinner)
PARIS: *8 APR → 21 MAY 1927
   2 Square Robiac: *8 Apr → 21 May 1927

HOLLAND: 21 MAY → 21 JUN 1927
    Hotel Victoria, The Hague : 21 May → 7 Jun 1927
        Scheveningen: 25 May 1927
    Hotel Krasnopolsky, Amsterdam: 7 Jun → 14 Jun 1927
    Hotel Victoria, The Hague: 14 Jun → 20 Jun 1927
    Hotel Central, Brussels: 20 Jun → 21 Jun 1927

PARIS: 21 JUN 1927 → *21 MAR 1928
    2, Square Robiac: 21 Jun 1927 → *21 Mar 1928
        (Joyce ill/depressed: Nov-Dec 1927)

NORMANDY: *21 MAR → 31 MAR 1928
    Hotel du Rhin et de Newhaven, Dieppe: *21 Mar → 27 Mar
        1928
    Grand Hôtel de la Poste, Rouen: 27 Mar → 31 Mar 1928

PARIS: 31 MAR → *19 APR 1928
    2 Square Robiac: 31 Mar → *19 Apr 1928

SOUTH OF FRANCE: *19 APR → 17 MAY 1928
    Dijon: *19 Apr → 20 Apr 1928
    Hotel Carlton, Lyon: 20 Apr → 21 Apr 1928
    Avignon: 21 Apr → 23 Apr 1928
    Grand Hotel, Toulon (Var): 23 Apr → 7 May 1928
    Hôtel d'Europe, Avignon: 7 May → 12 May 1928
    Hotel Carlton, Lyon: 12 May → 17 May 1928

PARIS: 17 MAY → *13 JUL 1928
    2, Square Robiac: 17 May → *13 Jul 1928

AUSTRIA: *13 JUL → 14 SEP 1928
    en route *13 Jul → *14 Jul 1928

Central Hotel, Zurich: *14 Jul → 15 Jul 1928
Hotel Europa, Innsbruck: 15 Jul → 23 Jul 1928
Hotel Mirabell, Salzburg: 23 Jul → 29 Aug 1928
Hotel Vier Jahreszejten, Munich: 29 Aug → 3 Sep 1928
Hôtel Maison Rouge, Strasburg: 3 Sep → *5 Sep 1928

NORMANDY: *5 SEP → 14 SEP 1928
   Paris *5 Sep 1928
   Hôtel Continental, Le Havre: *5 Sep → 14 Sep 1928

PARIS: 14 SEP 1928 → 10 JUL 1929
   2, Square Robiac: 14 Sep → *7 Nov 1928
   Maison de Santé, Neuilly: *7 Nov → *18 Nov 1928
      (Nora Joyce operation: 8 Nov 1928)
   2 Square Robiac: *18 Nov → 3 Dec 1928
   Maison de Santé, Neuilly: 3 Dec → 15 Dec 1928
      (Nora Joyce ill)
   2 Square Robiac: 15 Dec 1928 → *4 Feb 1929
   Maison de Santé, Neuilly: *4 Feb → **18 Feb 1929
      (Nora Joyce Op. Hysterectomy: 5 Feb 1929)
   2 Square Robiac: **18 Feb → 10 Jul 1929

SOUTH-WEST ENGLAND: 10 JUL → *19 SEP 1929
   Euston Hotel, London: 10 Jul → *14 Jul 1929
   Imperial Hotel, Torquay: *14 Jul → 14/15 Aug 1929
   Royal Hotel, Bristol: 14/15 Aug → 16/18 Aug 1929
   Euston Hotel, London: 16/18 Aug → *19 Sep 1929

PARIS: *19 SEP 1929 → *1 APR 1930
   2, Square Robiac: *19 Sep 1929 → *1 Apr 1930
      (Joyce prostrate first 3 weeks November 1929)

ZURICH/WIESBADEN: *1 APR → 21 APR 1930
 St Gotthard Hotel, Zurich: *1 Apr → 14 Apr 1930
  (Prof Vogt: consultation)
 Hotel Rose, Wiesbaden: 14 Apr → 21 Apr
  (Dr Panjenstecher: consultation)

PARIS: 21 APR → **13 MAY 1930
 2 Square Robiac: 21 Apr → **13 May 1930

ZURICH: **13 MAY → 17 JUN 1930
 St Gotthard Hotel, Zurich: **13 May → *14 May 1930
 Prof Vogt Clinic: *14 May → 5 Jun 1930
  (Eye OP. #9 (9): tertiary cataract left eye 15 May 1930)
 St Gotthard Hotel, Zurich: 5 Jun → 17 Jun 1930

PARIS: 17 JUN → *2 JUL 1930
 2 Square Robiac: 17 Jun → *2 Jul

WALES, ENGLAND: *2 JUL → **25 AUG 1930
 London: *2 Jul → 2/18 Jul 1930
 Grand Hotel, Llandudno: 2/18 Ju → *1 Aug 1930
 Randolph Hotel, Oxford: *1 Aug → *5 Aug 1930
 Somewhere in England: *5 Aug → **24 Aug 1930
 Lord Warden Hotel, Dover: **24 Aug → **25 Aug 1930

PARIS: **25 AUG → *29 AUG 1930
 2 Square Robiac: **25 Aug → *29 Aug 1930

NORTHERN FRANCE: *29 AUG → **14 SEP 1930
 Les Golf Hôtels (Hôtel de la Plage), Étretat: *29 Aug → **14
  Sep 1930

PARIS: **14 SEP → 23 NOV 1930
  2 Square Robiac: **14 Sep → 23 Nov 1930

ZURICH: 23 NOV → 27 NOV 1930
  Carlton Elite Hotel, Zurich: 23 Nov → 27 Nov 1930
    (Prof Vogt : Consultation)

PARIS: 27 NOV 1930 → *19 APR 1931
  2 Square Robiac: 27 Nov 1930 → 10 Apr 1931
  Hotel Powers: 10 Apr → 19 Apr 1931

LONDON: 19 APR → *24 SEP 1931
  Terminus-Hôtel, Calais: *19 Apr → 23 Apr 1931
  Hotel Belgravia, London: 23 Apr → 7/8 May 1931
  28b Campden Grove, London: 7/8 May → 7 Aug 1931
    (Joyce's "second" marriage: 4 Jul 1931)
  The Lord Warden Hotel, Dover: 7 Aug → 20/22 Aug 1931
  28B Campden Grove, London: 20/22 Aug → *29 Aug 1931
  Salisbury: *29 Aug → *1 Sep 1931
  28B Campden Grove, London: *1 Sep → *24 Sep 1931

PARIS: *24 SEP 1931 → 6 JUL 1932
  "La Résidence": *24 Sep → *9 Oct 1931
  2 Avenue S. Philibert: *9 Oct 1931 → 17 Apr 1932
  Hôtel Belmont: 17 Apr → *22 May 1932
    (Lucia collapse: Summer 1932)
  2 Avenue S. Philibert: *22 May → 6 Jul 1932

ZURICH, FELDKIRCH: 6 JUL → *19 SEP 1932
  Carlton Elite Hotel, Zurich : 6 Jul → 12/15 Aug 1932
    (Consultations Vogt: 11 Jul and 3 Aug 1932)
  Hotel zum Löwen, Feldkirch: 12/15 Aug → 8 Sep 1932

    (Liechtenstein: 18 Aug 1932)
    Carlton Elite Hotel, Zurich: 8 Sep → *19 Sep 1932
      (Consultation Vogt: 17 Sep 1932)

NICE: *19 SEP → *19 OCT 1932
    Hotel Metropole, Nice: *19 Sep → *19 Oct 1932

PARIS: *19 OCT 1932 → *22 MAY 1933
    Hotel Lord Byron: *19 Oct → 11/17 Nov 1932
    Hotel Lenox: 11/17 Nov → 17/25 Nov 1932
    42 rue Galilée: 17/25 Nov 1932 → *22 May 1933
      Rouen: mid-Jan 1933

ZURICH: *22 MAY → 10 JUN 1933
    Hotel Habis, Zurich: *22 May → 10 Jun 1933
      (Consultation Vogt)

PARIS: 10 JUN → *4 JUL 1933
    42, rue Galilée: 10 Jun → *4 Jul 1933

SWITZERLAND: *4 JUL → 28/31 AUG 1933
    Le Grand Hôtel, Évian-les Bains: *4 Jul → 10/12 Jul 1933
    Grand Hôtel de Russie, Geneva: 10/12 Jul → 13/17 Jul 1933
    St Gotthard Hotel, Zurich: 13/17 Jul → 22 Jul 1933
    Hotel Habis Royal, Zurich: 22 Jul → 30 Jul 1933
      Nyon: 30 Jul → 31 Jul
    Hôtel Richemond, Geneva: 31 Jul → 28/31 Aug 1933

PARIS: 28/31 AUG 1933 → *24 MAR 1934
    42 rue de la Galilée : 28/31 Aug 1933 → *24 Mar 1934

MONTE CARLO-NEUCHÂTEL-ZURICH (MOTOR-TOUR):
*24 MAR → 17/24 APR 1934
Lyons
Marseilles
Hôtel Heloer, Ventimiglia: 1 Apr 1934
Monte Carlo
Hôtel Moderne et des Trois Dauphins, Grenoble: 9 Apr 1934
Neuchatel
Carlton Elite Hotel, Zurich: *10 Apr → 18/24 Apr 1934
   (Consultation Vogt)

PARIS: 18/24 APR → *19 JUL 1934
   42 rue de la Galilée: 18/24 Apr → *19 Jul 1934
   Dieppe : 9 Jul 1934

BELGIUM, LUXEMBURG, SWITZERLAND: *19 JUL 1934 →
*1 FEB 1935
   Hotel Suede, Liège: 19 Jul → 20 Jul 1934
   Grand Hotel Britannique, Spa, Belgique: 20 Jul → 14/16 Aug
     1934
     Verviers: 14/16 Aug 1934
   Grand Hotel Brasseur, Luxembourg : 14/16 Aug → 22 Aug
     1934
   Basel: 22 Aug → 24/26 Aug 1934
   Grand Hotel Monney, Montreux: 24/26 Aug → 28 Aug/1 Sep
     1934
   Hôtel Richemonde, Geneva: 28 Aug/1 Sep → 2/5 Sep 1934
   Hôtel de la Paix, Geneva: 2/5 Sep → *20 Sep 1934
   Carlton Elite Hotel, Zurich: *20 Sep 1934 → *1 Feb 1935
     Neuhausen: 14 Oct 1934

PARIS: *1 FEB → 28 AUG/4 SEP 1935

"La Residence": *1 Feb → **11 Feb 1935
7 rue Edmond Valentin: **11 Feb → 31 Aug/4 Sep 1935

FONTAINBLEU: 31 AUG/4 SEP → *29 SEP 1935
   Savoy Hôtel, Fontainbleu: 31 Aug/4 Sep → 8/9 Sep 1935
   Hôtel de France, Versailles: 8/9 Sep → *17 Sep 1935
   Savoy Hotel, Fontainebleau: *17 Sep → *29 Sep 1935

PARIS: *29 SEP 1935 → *30 JUL 1936
   7 rue Edmond Valentin: *29 Sep 1935 → *30 Jul 1936

CENTRAL AND NORTHERN FRANCE: *30 JUL → 13/18
   AUG 1936
   Hôtel de l'Abbaye, Beaugency: *30 Jul → *8 Aug 1936
   Villa Connemara, Villers sur Mer: *8 Aug → 10 Aug 1936
   Casino de Deauville: 10 Aug → 13/18 Aug 1936

PARIS: 13/18 AUG → 18 AUG 1936
   7, rue Edmond Valentin: 13/18 Aug → 18 Aug 1936

DENMARK: 18 AUG → *13 SEP 1936
   Liège: 18 Aug → 19/21 Aug 1936
   Hotel Streit, Hamburg: 19/21 Aug → 22 Aug 1936
   Turist Hotel, Copenhagen: 22 Aug → 6 Sep 1936
     Elsinore, Denmark: 26 Aug 1936
   Hotel Streit, Hamburg: 6 Sep → 8 Sep 1936
   Cologne: 8 Sep → *10 Sep 1936
   Liége: *10 Sep → *13 Sep 1936

PARIS: *13 SEP 1936 → **1 APR 1937
   7 rue Edmond Valentin: *13 Sep 1936 → **1 Apr 1937

ZURICH: **1 APR → *17 APR 1937
   Carlton Elite Hotel, Zurich: **1 Apr → 17 Apr 1937

PARIS: 17 APR → *12 AUG 1937
   7 rue Edmond Valentin: 17 Apr → *12 Aug 1937

SWITZERLAND : *12 AUG → 1/4 SEP 1937
   Hôtel des Trois Rois, Basel: *12 Aug → 14 Aug 1937
   Hotel Krone am Rhein, Rheinfelden: 14 Aug → 21/25 Aug
     1937
   Carlton Elite Hotel, Zurich: 21/25 Aug → 1/4 Sep 1937

DIEPPE: 1/4 SEP → 14/15 SEP 1937
   Grand Hôtel, Dieppe: 1/4 Sep → 14/15 Sep 1937

PARIS : 14/15 SEP 1937 → *7 FEB 1938
   7 rue Edmond Valentin: 14/15 Sep 1937 → *7 Feb 1938

SWITZERLAND: *7 FEB → 28 FEB/8 MAR 1938
   Hôtel de la Paix, Lausanne: *7 Feb → 8/9 Feb 1938
   Carlton Elite Hotel, Zurich: 8/9 Feb → 28 Feb/8 Mar 1938

PARIS: 28 FEB/8 MAR → 20 AUG 1938
   7 rue Edmond Valentin: 28 Feb/8 Mar → 20 Aug 1938

SWITZERLAND: 20 AUG → *12 SEP 1938
   Hôtel de la Paix, Lausanne: 20 Aug → *12 Sep 1938
     Fribourg: 6 Sep 1938
   Dijon: *12 Sep 1938

PARIS: *12 SEP → 21 SEP 1938
   7 rue Edmond Valenti : *12 Sep → 21 Sep 1938

NORTHERN AND WESTERN FRANCE: 21 SEP → *3 OCT 1938
    Hôtel du Rhin et de Newhaven, Dieppe: 21 Sep → 27 Sep 1938
    Nante-gare: 27 Sep 1938
    Adelphi Hotel, La Baule: 28 Sep → *3 Oct 1938

PARIS: *3 OCT 1938 → *20 JUL 1939
    7 rue Edmond Valentin: *3 Oct 1938 → *15 Apr 1939
        Versailles: 2 Jan 1939
    Hôtel d'Iéna: *15 Apr → *24 Apr 1939
    34 rue des Vignes: *24 Apr → *20 Jul 1939

NORTHERN FRANCE: *20 JUL → *25 JUL 1939
    Les Golf Hotels, Étretat: *20 Jul → *25 Jul 1939

PARIS: *25 JUL → 7/10 AUG 1939
    34 rue des Vignes: *25 Jul → 7/10 Aug 1939

SWITZERLAND: 7/10 AUG → *25 AUG 1939
    Hôtel de la Paix, Lausanne: 7/10 Aug → 14 Aug 1939
    Hotel Schweizerhof, Bern: 14 Aug → *22 Aug 1939
    Grand Hôtel Monney, Montreux: *22 Aug → *25 Aug 1939

PARIS: *25 AUG → 28 AUG 1939
    34 rue des Vignes: *25 Aug → 28 Aug 1939

BRITTANY, FRANCE: 28 AUG → *14 OCT 1939
    Hôtel Majestic, La Baule: 28 Aug → 2 Sep 1939
    Hôtel St Christophe, La Baule: 2 Sep → *14 Oct 1939
    en route: *14 Oct → *15 Oct 1939

PARIS: *15 OCT → *23 DEC 1939
    Hôtel Lutétia: *15 Oct → *23 Dec 1940

ALLIER, FRANCE: *24 DEC 1939 → *22 JAN 1940
  Hôtel de la Paix, S Gérand-le-Puy : *24 Dec 1939 → *22 Jan 1940

PARIS: *22 JAN → *1 FEB 1940
  Hôtel Lutétia: *22 Jan → *1 Feb 1940

ALLIER, FRANCE: *1 FEB → 14 DEC 1940
  Hôtel de la Paix, S Gérand-le-Puy : *1 Feb → **28 Mar 1940
  Chateau de La Chapelle, Périguy: **28 Mar → **4 Apr 1940
  Hôtel Beaujolais, Vichy: **4 Apr → *16 Jun 1940
  Flat, S Gérand-le-Puy: *16 Jun → 10/28 Jul 1940
    (Arrival Paul Léon: 18 Jun 1940)
  Hôtel du Commerce, S. Gérand-le-Puy: 10/28 Jul → 28 Sep/13
    Oct 1940
    (Departure Maria Jolas: Aug 28 1940)
    (Departure Paul Léon: early Sep 1940)
  Maison Ponthenier. S. Gérand-le-Puy: 28 Sep/13 Oct → *14
    Dec 1940

SWITZERLAND: *14 DEC 1940 → 13 JAN 1941
  en route 14 Dec → *18 Dec 1940
  Lyons
  Hôtel Richemonde, Geneva: *14 Dec → *15 Dec 1940
  Hôtel de la Paix, Lausanne: *15 Dec → 17 Dec 1940
  Pension Delphin, Zurich 17 Dec 1940 → 10 Jan 1941
  Schwesterhaus vom Roten Kreuz, Zurich: 10 Jan → 15 Jan
    1941
    (*Obit*: 2.15 a.m. 13 Jan 1941)
  Fluntern Cemetery, Zurich: 15 Jan 1941
    (Joyce's body was moved to a new grave in 1966.)

Appendix B: publication of Work in progress 1924-1939

A Chronological List

Early versions of most of the constituent parts of *Work in progress* appeared in little magazines and/or booklet form in the period 1924-1938. *Finnegans wake* was published on 4 May 1939. In the following list (which does not, of course, include translations or excerpts printed in critical articles) I have appended to each entry the corresponding section of *Finnegans wake* and the date (sometimes approximate) of publication.

Transatlantic review I-4: II.4 (FW 383-399), *c.* 1 April 1924

In *Contact collection of contemporary writers*, ed. Robert McAlmon: I.2§1 (FW 30-34.29), *c.* 1 Jun 1925

Criterion III-12: I.5 (FW 104-125), *c.* 21 Jul 1925

Two worlds 1: I.5 (FW 104-125), September 1925

Navire d'argent I-5: I.8 (FW 196-216), *c.* 1 Oct 1925

This quarter I-2: I.7 (FW 169-195), Nov 1925

Two worlds 2: I.2§1 (FW 30-34.29), December 1925

Two worlds 3: I.8 (FW 196-216), March 1926

Two worlds 4: I.7 (FW 169-195), June 1926

Two worlds 5: II.4 (FW 383-399), September 1926

transition 1: I.1 (FW 3-29), *c.* 1 Apr 1927

transition 2: I.2 (FW 30-47), *c.* mid Apr 1927

transition 3: I.3 (FW 48-74), *c.* mid May 1927

transition 4: I.4 (FW 75-103), *c.* mid Jun 1927

transition 5: I.5 (FW 104-125), *c.* mid Jul 1927

transition 6: I.6 (FW 126-168), *c.* end Aug 1927

transition 7: I.7 (FW 169-195), *c.* end Sep 1927

transition 8: I.8 (FW 196-216), *c.* beginning Nov 1927

transition 11: II.2§8 (FW 282.05-304.04), Feb 1928

transition 12: III.1 (FW 403-428), *c.* 21 Mar 1928

transition 13: III.2 (FW 429-473), *c.* 13 Jul 1928

transition 15: III.3 (FW 474-554), early Feb 1929

Anna Livia Plurabelle (Crosby Gaige): I.8 (FW 196-216), 29 Oct 1928

Tales told of Shem and Shaun (Black Sun Press): I.6§3, II.2§8 and III§IC (FW 152.04-159.23, 282.05-304.04 and 414.22-419.10), *c.* Aug 1929

In *transition stories* ed. Eugene Jolas and Robert Sage: I.2§1 and fragments of I.4, I.3, III.2, III.1, I.1 and I.3 (FW 30-34.29, 76.33-78.06, 65.05-24, 454.26-455.29, 413.03-26, 23.16-26, 74.13-19). 1929

transition 18: III.4 (FW 555-590), Nov 1929

Haveth childers everywhere (Babou and Kahane): ca. mid-Apr 1930

Anna Livia Plurabelle (Faber and Faber): I.8 (FW 196-216), 1 May 1930

In *Imagist anthology 1930*, ed. Richard Aldington: fragment of III.1 (FW 417.24-419.10), May 1930

Haveth childers everywhere (Faber and Faber): 2 Apr 1931

Two tales of Shem and Shaun (Faber and Faber): I.6§3 and III§IC (FW 152.04-159.23 and 414.22-419.10), 24 November 1932

transition 22: II.1 (FW 219-259), 21 Feb 1933

Les amis de 1914 40: fragment of II.1 (FW 258.25-259), 23 Feb 1934

The mime of Mick, Nick and the Maggies (The Servire Press): II.1 (FW 219-259), *c.* 1 Jun 1934

transition 23: II.2§1,2,3 and 9 (FW 260-275.02, 304.05-308), 6 Jul 1935

transition 26: II.3§1 (FW 309-331), *c.* 1 May 1937

Storiella as she is syung (Corvinus Press): II.2§1,2,3 and 9 (FW 260-275.02, 304.05-308), *c.* 28 Feb 1938

Verve I-2: II.1 (fragment: FW 244.13-246.02), Mar 1938

transition 27: II.3§4-5 (FW 338.04-355.07), mid May 1938

Finnegans wake (Faber and Faber, London; The Viking Press, New York): 4 May 1939